THE FREQUENCY OF SUCCESS

How to Master Manifestation Through the Law of Vibration

By
Steve Linton

The Frequency of Success:
How to Master Manifestation Through the Law of Vibration

Written by Steve Linton
© 2025 by Steve Linton

Paperback ISBN: 978-1-967587-78-0
eBook ISBN: 978-1-967587-79-7

All rights reserved. No part of this book may be reproduced in whole or part, or used in any matter without express written permission from the author—except for brief quotations in a book review.

This book is a work of nonfiction. It represents the accuracy of the events mentioned to the best of the author's recollection. Some names in the book have been replaced to maintain the privacy of certain individuals.

The information contained in this book is provided for educational purposes only and should not be construed as legal, financial, tax, or investment advice. Readers are strongly encouraged to consult with a qualified and licensed professional who can provide advice tailored to their individual circumstances. Laws, regulations, and financial practices vary across countries, states, and regions. Market conditions, returns, and outcomes will differ over time and cannot be guaranteed. While every effort has been made to provide accurate and timely information at the time of writing, we make no representations or warranties regarding completeness, accuracy, or applicability. We are not making any official legal or financial recommendations. The examples, figures, and principles presented herein are for illustrative and educational purposes only. Any decisions you make are solely your responsibility.

To my father, whose love of aviation lifted my dreams skyward. Though you left us in 1997, just as my professional flying career was taking flight, your influence soars through every hour I've logged and every airplane I've commanded. As a pilot and air traffic controller, you didn't just teach me to fly—you taught me to see the world from a higher perspective. I wish you could have witnessed the journey: the bigger airplanes, the captain's stripes, the 17,000 jumps into open sky. You would have been proud. I carry your spirit with me at every altitude.

To my sister, Lori, whose unwavering strength and grace have been my compass since childhood. You've inspired me through every chapter of my life, showing me what it means to live with integrity and purpose. Looking up to you has always kept me reaching higher.

To my wife, Mercedes, my rock and my light. On the days when the clouds roll in, you help me find the sun. You turn my struggles into strength and my doubts into determination. Your ability to see the positive in any situation has taught me more about the frequency of success than any book could capture. You make the journey worth taking.

This book is built on the foundation you three have given me—a father who taught me to fly, a sister who taught me to aspire, and a wife who teaches me to rise.

TABLE OF CONTENTS

Introduction 1
    Overcome Fear to Raise Your Frequency 6
    What Can a Skydiver Teach You About Success? 6
    How to Amplify Your Results With My FLIGHT Method 8
    Join the Frequency of Success Facebook Community 9

PART 1: THE FREQUENCY SHIFT: WHY YOUR ENERGY DETERMINES YOUR SUCCESS

CHAPTER 1: The Energy Equation—Your Results Mirror Your Energy 13

CHAPTER 2: Tune In to Find Your Frequency 25

CHAPTER 3: The 12 Universal Laws—Your Foundation for Vibrational Success 41

CHAPTER 4: Overcoming Turbulence—Three Obstacles to Watch Out For 57

CHAPTER 5: The 4 Foundational Pre-FLIGHT Practices 81

CHAPTER 6: The Missing Frequency 103

PART 2: THE FREQUENCY OF SUCCESS FRAMEWORK

CHAPTER 7: The FLIGHT Method 115

CHAPTER 8: Practices That Sustain High-Frequency Living 127

PART 3: HOW TO RAISE YOUR FREQUENCY

CHAPTER 9: Clear the Interference 149

CHAPTER 10: Simplify Your Signal 165

CHAPTER 11: Activate Your Frequency 175

CONCLUSION: Ready to Take FLIGHT 185

This Is Your Pilot Speaking 197

About the Author: Steve Linton 199

INTRODUCTION

Before we dive into frequencies and universal laws, I'd like to take you on a little adventure. During this adventure, you might feel a range of emotions: uncertainty, anxiety, discomfort, exhilaration, joy, or maybe even fear.

All of these emotions are perfectly normal—there is no right or wrong way to feel. I want you to simply immerse yourself in the experience.

Imagine that you're sitting in the passenger seat of my truck, watching the scenery go by as we drive down the interstate. You have no idea where we're going, but since we're friends, you trust me and are excited for the adventure.

As we approach our destination, I ask you to close your eyes. I don't want to ruin the surprise!

"We're almost there!" I say. "Just a little farther."

We make a couple of turns and then slow to a stop. I put the truck in park and cut the engine.

"Keep your eyes closed. I'll come help you out."

"OK," you say. You sound a bit nervous. Maybe you don't like surprises after all.

I open your door. "You're gonna love this!" I say as I help you out.

"I hope so," comes your reply. Do I hear a hint of uncertainty in your voice?

I guide you up the sidewalk and then ask you to stop.

"Open your eyes! We're here!"

You open your eyes and find that you're standing in front of a small building. The first thing you see is a sign with a parachute on it and the word "skydive." You look around and notice a couple of small planes. You think, *Oh no, no, no, no! This can't be happening!*

"I'm taking you skydiving!" I exclaim.

At this point, I understand if you're a little nervous. You might be feeling some anxiety. But I assure you, everything will be okay. I have over 31 years of experience in the sport and over 17,000 jumps, so I know you're going to be just fine.

I guide you through the front doors to the reception desk and hand you a clipboard with paperwork and a pen.

"I just need your ID and your signature here…and here." Your eyes are drawn to the statement in the waiver that says, "By signing this waiver, you acknowledge that skydiving is a dangerous activity and can result in injury or DEATH."

"Wait…what? Death?"

In the next room, I introduce you to Dean, your tandem master, and hand you a blue jumpsuit and a harness. You notice the round patch sewn onto the chest of the jumpsuit featuring an open parachute.

After your instructor helps you get suited up, you sit on the bench and watch a group of skydivers come in from the landing area. Your brows are furrowed with worry, and your stomach threatens to empty its contents onto the floor.

"Are you ready?" You startle at the sound of my voice. "We're going to take a tram down to the plane. As we approach the plane, I want you to stay right next to me so I can be sure you don't walk into the prop, okay?" The word DEATH flashes across the front of your brain like a neon sign.

"Okay," you say. You listen intently as I continue with the instructions.

"Watch your head when you go up the steps so you don't smack it on the floater bar. I won't be able to talk to you once we get on the plane because we won't be sitting together. You and Dean will sit up front, near the pilot, as we taxi out and take off. Once we get to altitude, the team will let you know when it's our turn to jump. Once we jump, I'm going to be right in front of you during the freefall, so don't forget to smile! Look around and enjoy the view. Did you get all that?"

"Watch my head…jump…smile…freefall?" The words sound distant, like they're coming from someone else. "Is it too late to back out?" you stammer.

Possibility of death! The words echo in your head as you wrangle with overwhelming fear and anxiety…now at a level ten and climbing.

You look like you're about to lose your lunch again. I clap you on the shoulder and smile. "This is gonna be great!" However, the expression on your face says something much different.

As the plane climbs through 10,000 feet on the way to 14,000 feet, I look down the bench at you. You look like you're contemplating every life decision you have ever made—especially this one.

The yellow light comes on, alerting us that we are less than one minute from opening the door. You see it, too, and tense up. A skydiver next to me yells, "Door!" as the five-foot-wide, roll-up door of the Twin Otter jump ship flies open and a rush of cold air fills the cabin. It's intense. Actually, you decide, it's beyond intense. You yell, "Wait, wait, wait…" but the wind whips the words away as soon as they leave your mouth.

You and Dean slide toward the door. Your eyes are wide and fixated. The wind noise is practically deafening. I lean in and yell, "Are you ready to skydive?"

No answer comes back. Your blank stare is so familiar. I've seen this look hundreds of times. It's what makes the whole adventure worthwhile.

I swing myself outside the airplane onto the camera step. Looking back at you and Dean, I see that your face is as pale as a sheet. It's like you've retreated to some faraway place and complete fear has stepped in to take control.

Dean starts his exit rock. Ready…set…go! He gives you a somersault exit as we leave the plane in unison. Dean deploys the drogue—a small, round parachute used to stabilize tandem skydivers—and I fly on my back up in front of you.

We're traveling through the atmosphere at 120 miles per hour! It's exhilarating! I position myself directly in front of and slightly below you so I can see your face. We're only about ten seconds out of the plane, and already your fear has melted away to reveal a grin from ear to ear. *Fear is gone, and in its place is fearlessness!*

You are a completely different person from the terrified you who clung to the airplane for dear life. Flying around the sky, you give me a thumbs up and a huge smile.

As we approach the landing, I hear you yell, "Woo-hoo!" You wave and laugh as you float down from the sky. It's a beautiful sight. "That was exhilarating! It's intoxicating!"

You and Dean complete an impeccable stand-up landing, and before I can even say a word, you yell, "That was incredible! It was so much better than I thought it would be. I want to go again!"

"So…you enjoyed it?"

"Oh my gosh! It was so cool! I didn't feel like I was falling or anything! Watching you fly around was awesome—I didn't know you could fly like that! We were actually flying!"

I congratulate you on your first-ever skydive and welcome you to a whole new world.

Overcome Fear to Raise Your Frequency

You may be wondering, "What does skydiving have to do with raising my frequency and becoming more successful?"

Skydiving is just one example of something that most people fear. Fear is the number one thing holding you back from success. Fear keeps you in mediocrity—stuck in a rut and living the same ordinary, unexceptional life day after day after day. And it affects all aspects of your life: personal, professional, and spiritual.

One thing to note about this story is the level of fear present at the beginning versus the end. The reason fear is not present at the end is simply because all the doubts, fears, negative thoughts, and apprehension were simply an illusion. You realize you can truly fly relative to something else in actual free fall. All of the stuff you created in your head about skydiving is just that—stuff you created! *None of it is reality.*

Throughout your life, you'll have many opportunities to metaphorically go skydiving. When these opportunities present themselves, what will you do? Will you shrink in fear? Or will you FLY?

What Can a Skydiver Teach You About Success?

You probably picked up this book because you want to learn how to raise your frequency to a level of success. You're wondering how you can be one of the "lucky" ones who seem to have it all figured out. You've tried so many things—the affirmations, the meditations, the visualizations—but nothing seemed to work for you...until now!

As I said before, fear is the number one thing holding you back. Fear is a very low-frequency emotion and to be successful, you must tap into higher vibrational frequencies. I'm going to show you exactly how to do that.

I wrote this book to teach you how to apply the universal laws and principles of frequency to your life. When you apply these principles, you'll see positive changes in areas like finance, business, health, relationships, and more.

I can show you how the universal laws work and how to apply them, but I can't do it for you. *You* are the only one who can do that. You have an innate knowledge of your unique talents and abilities and what's possible for you when you raise your frequency. Because at some level, maybe deep down, you already know what you're capable of. Understanding and applying the principles will help you improve and advance your abilities faster than you ever thought possible.

The truth is, I fought these concepts for a long time; I just didn't believe they had any real power. But I recognized that all of the successful people I knew had one thing in common: They were all practicing and applying these principles in their everyday lives, including their businesses and relationships.

It was then that I made the decision to truly apply them in my own life and business. It didn't take long for me to see the absolute power they held. Applying these concepts brought a fulfilling balance throughout every aspect of my life. It felt like having my own spiritual team guiding me through business and life decision-making.

While the concepts in this book are not new, it was born from my personal experience from putting them into practice to reach many achievements, including making over $100,000 in one month. More on that later, but for now, just know that if you keep reading, you'll learn how to tap into higher frequencies to accomplish more in every aspect of your life and experience success on every level—not just financially. Imagine what you can accomplish! *You* can be one of the "lucky" ones who have it all figured out. All you have to do is listen, learn, and apply these principles.

How to Amplify Your Results With My FLIGHT Method

In the pages to follow, I'll introduce you to my FLIGHT Method. It's a six-part method that, when applied consistently, will raise your vibration and amplify your results like never before!

You'll learn how to:

- Identify your current energy state
- Overcome old conditioning and release limiting beliefs
- Intentionally raise your vibration
- Take daily actions to stabilize high-frequency living
- Achieve inner balance
- Build momentum and witness profound life changes

We'll discuss the common symptoms of low-frequency living and how to cure them. You'll discover why the comparison trap lowers your vibration and derails your progress. And you'll find out how to spot the external influences in your life that can either drain your energy or raise your vibration.

When you leave fear behind and raise your frequency, you will be surprised at how quickly positive things start to happen for you. But if there's one thing you take away, it's that you have to commit to being consistent. Consistency is the key to making the FLIGHT Method work for you.

It doesn't matter who you are or where you start—the most important thing is to start today. It's okay to start small. In fact, I recommend it because each little win raises your frequency just a tiny bit. And that's all you need to create momentum and lift. Not only will you take flight, but you will enthusiastically soar every day!

Are you ready for takeoff?

Join the Frequency of Success Facebook Community

Everything that happens in life is affected by your energy and the frequency at which you operate. One of the best ways to raise your frequency is to be around people operating at a higher frequency than you. This book will show you how to raise your vibration intentionally, and it's a great place to start, but to get there faster, you need to surround yourself with like-minded people.

That's why I'm inviting you to join the Frequency of Success Facebook community. In this community, you'll find people just like you. People who once let fear rule their lives but now intentionally commit to raising their frequencies, live a life of purpose, choose gratitude, and recognize the vibrational changes that allow them to take flight in all areas of their life, one little win at a time. You will instantly feel the high frequency of this amazing group whether you simply read and learn from the posts and comments or choose to participate in the flight.

Part 1

THE FREQUENCY SHIFT: WHY YOUR ENERGY DETERMINES YOUR SUCCESS

What I originally thought was just a bunch of hocus pocus actually turned out to be incredibly powerful stuff.

CHAPTER 1

The Energy Equation—Your Results Mirror Your Energy

I spent almost $100,000 on five years of college and all of my flight training to fulfill my dream of becoming a professional pilot. The only problem was that the job market for pilots was horrible when I graduated. I felt pretty lucky when I landed my first job as a charter pilot, making less than $15,000 a year to fly people all around the country.

As you might imagine, I was living from day-to-day, paycheck-to-paycheck. I had spent all that money on college thinking I would earn a huge salary as a pilot—only to graduate and make $408 every two weeks. I was beyond bitter and extremely frustrated, and I had no idea how I was going to fix my situation.

I was angry at anyone and everyone for the fact that I was broke and going nowhere fast. My life was a never-ending treadmill of working for a pittance and struggling to cover my bills. I couldn't go on like this. I was barely surviving. Something had to change. I had to do something about my situation. But what?

That's when I started paying closer attention to something my friend had been talking about for the past few months. At first, I thought it was just weird, so I ignored him. But eventually, I figured I might as well give it a chance—things couldn't get any worse than my circumstances at that moment, and I could see his life was improving. So I began to listen and test the principles and techniques that he was talking about. I wanted proof that they worked.

Within a few weeks of applying the principles, I began to see not only changes in myself and my results, but also changes in how other people treated me and responded to me.

It was incredible! Why hadn't I done this sooner? It seemed so easy. Why wasn't everyone doing this? I was amazed at how fast everything in my life was changing. Every month that went by just kept getting better and better.

So what did I change? What did I do to suddenly bring success into my life after being stuck in a rut for so long?

It turns out my friend wasn't weird after all. It all comes down to a simple law of physics and a basic understanding of energy and vibration.

Energy and Vibration

To better understand the concepts that I'll be discussing in this book, it's helpful to have some familiarity with the laws of the universe. There is really only one law: *Energy is.* This law has several subsidiary laws, which I'll cover later, but for now, I'll give you a simple introduction to the concepts of energy and frequency.

The law, energy is, may sound somewhat incomplete, and you may ask yourself, "Energy is…what? What is energy?"

The easiest way to answer this is to say that energy is everything, and it is nothing. It's what fuels everything in the universe from the tiniest unseen atom to the largest star system. You can use different forms of energy, but it can be considered "nothing" because you can't see it, touch it, or hold it. Energy is not something you can bottle up and sell.

Let me give you an example of the room I am currently sitting in while I write. I can say it is a big room, or I can say it is a small room. The truth is that the room is neither big nor small. The room just is. Something cannot be big or small until we compare it to something else. Energy cannot be big or small, good or bad, hot or cold. Energy just is. Everything is only big or small relative to something else. If there were nothing to compare it to, energy would just be. Period.

In life, nothing happens by chance or coincidence. Everything happens by law. When you understand this simple concept, your level of awareness rises, your mind opens, and you begin to realize more success in your life.

Your thoughts, words, and actions are energy. You create manifestations through thoughts, words, and actions that use energy to form objects, conditions, and experiences. All the success and knowledge that ever was and ever will be is already here. All you have to do is condition your mind to begin to raise your level of awareness so you can realize it in physical form.

Everything in the universe and beyond is some form of matter. Think of everything you can touch, taste, see, and hear—it's all simply a form of matter that vibrates at a particular frequency.

Vibration (Frequency)

Now that you know a little more about energy, let's talk about frequency. Frequency is the speed at which things vibrate, meaning it's how often something happens, or repeats, over a period of time.

For example, the number of times your heart beats per minute is its frequency. Or the number of sound waves that pass a certain point in one second is its frequency. Higher-frequency sound waves produce higher-pitched sounds. For instance, a whistle has a higher frequency than a bass note.

When we talk about frequency and energy together, the higher the frequency, the higher the energy. Many things can cause your energy to change or "shift." You have conscious control over most of these things, like the food you eat, the drinks you consume, the music you listen to, the people you spend time with, and the thoughts and feelings you have.

What you may not realize is that everything you take into your body and conscious mind affects your energy. Every second of every day, you are constantly bombarded with waves of energy from light, sound, thoughts, actions, and experiences. These energy waves range in frequency from very low to very high.

Thought energy is the highest frequency of all forms of energy. Your conscious mind acts as a gatekeeper, choosing what to let into your subconscious mind. This ultimately determines your vibration, which also dictates your "mood" at any given moment.

Your Vibration Directly Affects Your Outcomes

Remember when I mentioned that I graduated from college and flight school, then got a job as a charter pilot making only $408 every two weeks? I was resentful and had a big chip on my shoulder. I felt I had been dealt a raw deal, especially after the amount of time and effort I put into my education.

In those days, weeks, and months, I was operating at a very low frequency. I was stuck in low-energy purgatory. No drive, just plodding along, hoping something would change while not doing anything to make a change. I felt frustrated, stagnated, and burned out. It was low-frequency living at its finest.

What I didn't know was that every negative thought I had, every payday pity party I threw, and every cynical and pessimistic comment I uttered only made my situation worse.

Most energy influence sources you face on a daily basis are somewhat constant, or at least predictable. For example, when you turn on the news, whether it's TV, radio, or social media, the energy influence you feel from them will be tipped more on the negative side. But if you pick up a personal development or self-help book, you'll find yourself in a positive or high-frequency energy influence.

Let's do another example. You're cruising down the highway when you see flashing blue and red lights ahead. You slow down and realize traffic is backed up and being diverted because of a rollover accident.

In version one of this story, you throw your hands up in frustration. "OMG! Now I have to find an alternate route, and I'm going to be late for work!" In version two, you say, "Thank goodness I wasn't part of that terrible accident! I hope no one was seriously injured. What a scary thing for everyone involved."

In the first version, you exude negative energy, which only breeds more negative energy. You'll probably hit several more "roadblocks" throughout your day with that negative attitude.

In the second version, you feel gratitude that you weren't involved in the accident and empathy for those who were—both positive emotions. You can't be negative when your mind is in a state of gratitude. When you carry positive energy with you throughout the day, you're happier and life seems to go well. This is positive energy and high-frequency living at its best!

Energetic Wildcard: People

The one unpredictable wild card in the onslaught of energy influence is people. The people you come in contact with, and who influence your energy, range from extremely negative (low frequency) to very positive (high frequency).

This is where it is critical to be exceptionally diligent about who you spend time with. Your success depends on it! We already know that everyone is made up of a mass of matter that vibrates at a given frequency. But is it possible that one person's energy could affect another's energy? Absolutely.

Spending time with negative people who vibrate at a low frequency is one of the primary reasons you don't reach your goals. You're constantly being sabotaged by the negative energy of the people you hang out with. Since thoughts, words, and actions are all energy, it makes sense that someone with a negative attitude or negative actions (both low-frequency vibrations) could bring someone who is vibrating on a higher frequency down to a much lower level.

Here's an example to illustrate how this happens. Let's say you have a cup of very hot water, and this represents a person with a high-frequency vibration. Then you fill another cup with very cold water. The cold water represents a person with a very low-frequency vibration.

What happens when you dump the cold water into the warm water? The very hot water is *brought down* to a much lower temperature, and the very cold water is *brought up* to a warmer temperature.

Since the hot water represents a person with a high-frequency vibration, adding the cold water, or low-frequency vibration, lowers that person's frequency.

This "energy contamination" happens in a number of ways that you may not even suspect. You go through your day-to-day life without even realizing that, despite your best efforts or intentions, you're being sabotaged by family, friends, coworkers, and in many cases, yourself. And you don't even know it.

What Happens When You Operate at a Higher Frequency?

While it's true that low-frequency people can drain energy from people operating at a higher frequency, the opposite is also true. A person with a high vibration can bring a person with a low vibration up to a higher level. This kind of person is very rare and usually extraordinarily skilled at energy control. These are typically personal development coaches, mentors, or healers.

When I finally decided to listen to my friend and give his ideas a shot, it was like a whole new world opened up to me. He was living at a higher frequency, and as I implemented the simple techniques he taught me, I began to raise my frequency to match his. Suddenly, opportunities came knocking and doors began to open.

I was amazed at how fast my life was changing. Every month, I set new personal and business goals that seemed impossible to reach. Did I hit my goals, on target, each month? Of course not, but I recognized a shift. I was growing. My life was changing for the better, and I began to see things differently. Every month, my belief expanded into a new realm, and I began experiencing staggering paradigm shifts in the levels of success that I could achieve.

What I didn't mention before was that at this time, I was in a 100% commission sales business where my income was solely dependent on me and my efforts alone. My paycheck was determined by the amount of sales I made. As you could guess, in my negative frequency, I wasn't doing so well. I hadn't given up on my dream of becoming a successful pilot; I still flew every chance I could get. But I needed income and the sales business helped bring in money I was sorely lacking.

After about three months of using the techniques my friend taught me, I achieved an income in only one month that equaled what many people made in an entire year at that time: $31,000.

That was bigger than anything I could have ever imagined, but as I said, each month, my paradigms shifted, and my belief in what was possible expanded exponentially.

The next month, I reached an income of just over $50,000 in only 30 days! Remember, I was not punching a time clock. This was 100% commissioned sales and solely dependent on me and my efforts.

One evening that month, I sat in a room filled with approximately 120 people, all listening to a live business presentation given by my business partner. During the presentation on what was possible in this business opportunity, he casually pointed at me.

"This guy just made over $50,000 in one month."

Of course, some people in the crowd were visibly skeptical. I would have been, too, if I hadn't done it myself.

But I hadn't even considered the possibility of what he said next.

He pointed to me and said, "Now watch this guy because in the next few months, you're going to see him make over $100,000 in one month."

At that very moment, he gave me possibly the biggest gift I will ever receive in my life. He gave me the gift of limitless belief.

My business partner didn't know it at the time, but he had planted the seed of possibility, and that seed grew like a weed. It only took about 30 seconds from the time he uttered those words for me to realize—yes! This was absolutely possible!

I didn't need to know *how* it would happen. All that mattered was that my belief system instantaneously expanded to a new level, and my subconscious mind now knew without a doubt that my potential was limitless.

By opening my mind to the possibilities, I raised my frequency. And the very next month, I generated a profit of $103,000 in 30 days.

Brace Yourself for a Paradigm Shift

Now, you might be feeling like some of those audience members—skeptical and disbelieving. My old self would have certainly felt that way. But remember, you picked up this book for a reason. Something about it resonated with you. Something nudged you to take a chance, to see what it was all about. Instead of thinking low-frequency thoughts like, "Yeah, sure. That's great, but that could never happen for me," what if you started operating at a higher frequency today?

Can you think of a few examples in your life where you could turn a negative thought or situation into a positive one? For example, if you consider yourself to be a procrastinator, imagine setting aside time each day to work on your project. See yourself taking accountability, doing the work, and celebrating your accomplishment. Make a goal to spend at least 30 minutes a day on your project. The next time you feel like procrastinating, remember your goal and get to work.

Another negative thought you might have could be about your health. Maybe you tell yourself that you are overweight, unhealthy, and always will be. Next time you have that thought, visualize yourself taking a walk. Think about how good the sunshine and fresh air feel as your lungs expand and your muscles loosen. Make a goal to walk for 15 minutes every day for the next month. Any time negative thoughts about your health creep in, let them go and replace them with positive thoughts about eating healthy food and getting exercise.

Now it's your turn. What are some of your loudest negative thoughts? Write them down and then open your mind, raise your frequency, and watch the magic happen.

You see, our thoughts, feelings, and actions are interconnected. Thoughts are the catalyst that directly influence emotions, and emotions are what drive actions. It's a cycle: beliefs and thoughts become feelings, which lead to actions. If you want results, you have to take action.

Once I let go of negative thinking and opened my mind to the possibilities, I went on to have several six-figure months, each being bigger than the last. I changed my belief, and I took action. But the best part? I shared this same information—the same method I'm teaching you in this book—with hundreds of people who went on to shatter my income records and achieve astounding success.

So I Ask, "Why Not You?"

The good news is you're well on your way. Just by reading this far, you've already begun to open your mind and invite higher frequencies and positive energy into your life. The great news is that when you start to make even the smallest changes in your life on a daily basis, you will see positive and transformational changes over time.

What I've learned over the past 20 years can be summed up in one simple sentence: *Your success in life is limited only by your beliefs*. Read that again! You hold the key to achieving any result you desire. It all comes down to your vibration. That's the key to your success.

Have you ever heard the phrase: You get what you focus on? If you want more positivity in your life, then start focusing on becoming more positive. If you want more income, then stop saying that you never have enough money. Instead, flip the script and start believing you have more than you need.

In the next chapter, we're going to dive a little deeper into why these principles are available to anyone and everyone, including you. I'll show you how to recognize when you're operating at a low vibrational state and how to identify frequency patterns in your life history.

One of my favorite sayings is: *The only way to FAIL is to QUIT.* So let's keep going!

CHAPTER 2

Tune In to Find Your Frequency

A small handful of men turn their coat collars up against the wind as it sweeps across the dunes of Kitty Hawk, North Carolina. Shivering in the early morning light, they gather around an oversized mechanical apparatus made of muslin fabric pulled taut around a wooden frame. Two large wings, one over the other, are connected by a framework of posts and wires. A small 12-horsepower engine, housed in a light aluminum crankcase and attached to the lower wing, powers two propellers on either side of the back of the plane. There are no wheels. Linear skids act as landing gear.

The Wright brothers take their positions with Orville lying prone over the lower wing. He slips the restraining rope loose, and the bulky contraption inches forward down the takeoff rail and into a fierce headwind. Wilbur walks alongside, one hand on the wing. At the end of the track, the Flyer lifts—and history is made.

For 12 seconds, Orville experiences, in his words, an "extremely erratic" flight as the machine rises and dips like a "bucking bronco." Then, one wing strikes the sand and brings the plane to a bumpy stop. The total distance in the air is 120 feet.

This seemingly flimsy apparatus was a biplane, known now as the Wright Flyer. The men gathered that fateful morning of December 17, 1903, and witnessed 12 seconds that would change the world forever.[1]

Three more powered flights were achieved that day, each one gaining additional distance over the one before. The fourth and final flight measured 852 feet with a flight time of 59 seconds.

You Don't Need Perfect Conditions

Although the story of the Wright Flyer and the first powered flight might be the most famous of the Wright brothers' flights today, people at the time were extremely skeptical. Only a handful of men were actually there to witness the feat, and newspapers initially published the story with wildly inaccurate information.[2] [3]

---

[1] National Air and Space Museum, "The Wright Brothers Made History at Kitty Hawk," June 23, 2022, https://airandspace.si.edu/stories/editorial/wright-brothers-made-history-kitty-hawk#:~:text=At%2010:35%20a.m.%2C%20on,852%20feet%20in%20 59%20seconds.

[2] "1903 Commemorative Sculpture (U.S. National Park Service)." National Parks Service. Accessed January 7, 2026. https://www.nps.gov/places/000/december-17-1903.htm#:~:text=The%20sculpture%20includes:%20*%20**W.C.%20 Brinkley**%20A,Wright%20brothers%20in%20their%20later%201908%20flights.

[3] "When the Wright Brothers Shocked the World, the Dayton Media Flubbed It." Dayton Daily News, December 17, 2025. https://www.daytondailynews.com/news/local/throwback-thursday-when-the-wright-brothers-shocked-the-world-and-the-media-flubbed/dKLdhFWlSUevZE6wR22GmJ/.

But that did not stop these enterprising men. They went on to refine their design and develop a two-passenger airplane, which they demonstrated in both Europe and the US. Their ingenuity laid the foundation for modern aviation and secured their place in history.

In every experiment, they defined what success would look like. Each success raised their frequency and that of other aviation and aeronaut enthusiasts. Just reading their story instills the hope that what was once impossible is now possible.

The Wright brothers had a vision: They believed powered flight was possible, and they worked tirelessly to achieve it. They didn't wait until conditions were perfect, and they didn't let their early failures stop them from trying again.

Like Wilbur and Orville Wright, you don't need to have it all figured out to get off the ground. You just need to believe that you can.

That's what this book is here to help you do: design your version of flight, one belief, and one action at a time.

It's important to note that the Wright brothers did not invent flying. All of the knowledge that ever was or ever will be has always been here. We just have to raise our level of awareness in order to access that knowledge. The Wright brothers figured out how to put things in the right order for the airplane to actually fly. All they had to do was raise their level of awareness to discover *how* it could be done.

The same is true with the principles of energy, frequency, and vibration that I'm going to teach you in this book. They are not new, but when you raise your level of awareness and learn how to harness them, you'll feel like a new person who can soar to new heights.

What Does Success Mean to You?

Just like the Wright brothers defined what success looked like to them, you get to define what success looks like to you. This is a good time to consider such a profound thought.

I've worked hard to live my life by one guiding principle: The surest way to get anything you want in life is to help other people get what they want.

I want to help you get everything you want out of life. In turn, I'll get what I want. To me, that's what success is. Helping others raises *my* frequency, which attracts more of the good things life has to offer *me*.

The same can be true for you. Raising *your* frequency attracts more of the good things life has to offer *you*. So, what do you want out of your one beautiful life? What does *more* mean to you?

Is it financial freedom? A successful business? Stronger and deeper relationships with friends and family? Time with your kids or peace of mind?

Have you ever thought about what success looks like for you? Generally, success is thought of as a "favorable or desired outcome."

But your definition is personal. Remember, only you get to define what success looks like for you and what your outcome will be. And that's the most important part of this process.

It's true that the definition of "success" can be applied to virtually any area of your life, but it's a very individual thing. What success means for you should be defined by you and only you. Nobody else's idea of success matters. It's different for everyone, and it should be because we are each unique.

Too often, we adopt someone else's version of success without even realizing it. We chase shiny things because they're popular; it's what the "cool kids" are doing. We try so hard to "keep up with the Joneses" because we don't want to be left out or looked down upon.

In today's social scene, you'll notice that many people have a very shallow definition of success. Celebrities and influencers curate a highlight reel on social media, flaunting luxury automobiles, posh mansions, seven (or more) figures in the bank, and millions of followers.

Can all of these trappings be a legitimate part of success? Absolutely. But they aren't the whole picture, and they certainly aren't a guarantee of fulfillment. The result of chasing someone else's version of success is often heartbreak, misery, disappointment, and burnout.

Jim Rohn said, "If you don't design your own life, chances are you'll fall into someone else's plan. And guess what they have planned for you? Not much."[4]

---

[4] Jim Rohn, "15 of Jim Rohn's Most Motivational Quotes," *Jim Rohn Blog*, September 10, 2020, https://www.jimrohn.com/15-of-jim-rohns-most-motivational-quotes/.

Let that sink in.

You need to define success on your terms, based on your wants, desires, passion, and vision. Too many people follow the wrong dream—someone else's dream—without even realizing it.

Those who have achieved the greatest levels of true success are people who are not afraid to blaze their own trail. Rather than follow along just because it's popular, they are not afraid to fail. Like the Wright brothers, they persevere despite setback after setback. They have also honestly and authentically answered these three questions:

1. What makes me happy?
2. What am I passionate about?
3. How do I want to help people?

Remember that before we can help others, we need to help ourselves (self-improvement), which is why you're reading this book.

As you continue reading, let these questions linger in your mind. Your subconscious will quietly deliver the answers to you in the form of thoughts and ideas. Make sure to capture them as soon as they come to mind by jotting them down in a notebook. The act of writing with pen and paper is proven to be more powerful than just typing something on your computer or on your phone because the physical act of writing requires more cognitive processing. Handwriting activates more areas of the brain, enabling you to internalize your thoughts better, and allows your subconscious to work on your thoughts behind the scenes.[5] Once you begin to hear your own voice more clearly, you can start designing a life that aligns with it.

Your Frequency Is the Secret Formula

Here's a foundational truth of frequency: *Your frequency determines your results.*

Think of it this way: Frequency is like a radio station. If you want to listen to classic rock, you can't keep tuning in to jazz. If you want to experience success, you can't keep vibrating at the frequency of failure.

Frequency and results go hand in hand. It's a simple law of physics: like attracts like. High-frequency energy attracts high-frequency results. If you operate on a higher frequency, you'll attract more positive results.

The converse is also true. Low-frequency vibration attracts low-frequency results. This works in finance, business, relationships, or any aspect of life where you want to succeed.

It Takes More Than Positive Thinking

Some new-wave gurus would have you believe that all you need to do is start thinking positively. And while it's true that there is power in positive thinking, it is not enough to tip the scales.

To truly make a change, what you need is *belief* plus *action*.

Imagine this: You're strapped in your Jeep, driving down the trail, when you get stuck in a rut. The wheels start spinning,

---

5 Frederikus R. van der Weel and Audrey L. H. van der Meer, "Handwriting but Not Typewriting Leads to Widespread Brain Connectivity: A High-Density EEG Study with Implications for the Classroom," *Frontiers in Psychology* 14 (2023): article 1219945, https://doi.org/10.3389/fpsyg.2023.1219945

digging the vehicle deeper into the groove. But then you stop, turn on the 4-wheel drive, give it a little gas, and the Jeep effortlessly crawls out of the trench that had you trapped, enabling you to move forward. What's the difference? Traction.

In the world of frequency and vibration, positive thinking is like 2-wheel drive. It gets you to most places as long as you don't get stuck. When you switch to 4-wheel drive, you create enough traction to climb out. Shifting into 4-wheel drive is the catalyst; it's your belief. It gives you the traction you need when you step on the gas—the action. It's more than just positive thinking; it's *belief* plus *action*. And that's the traction you need to get unstuck.

Your Subconscious Mind Believes Everything You Tell It

I'm going to let you in on a little secret: Your subconscious doesn't know the difference between fact and fiction. It believes whatever you tell it, and then it will manifest those thoughts into physical reality.

If you tell it you're happy and healthy, it believes you.

If you tell it you're broke, sick, and underappreciated, it believes you.

Your subconscious mind informs your belief system. Positive thinking might make you feel better, but it won't help you get better results. You have to trick your subconscious mind into *believing* you already have the success you're after.

This is where affirmations and visualizations come into play. They aren't just wishful thinking. They can rewire your brain.

It's called neuroplasticity, and it works by strengthening the positive neural pathways to reshape your thought patterns.[6]

We'll talk more about meditation and mindfulness techniques later, but for now, I just want you to start playing with the idea that your subconscious believes what you tell it. Start acting and believing you already have what you're wishing for.

That may be easier said than done, so to help you out, I'm going to share a frequency self-assessment you can do right now.

What's Your Current Frequency?

Before you can raise your frequency, you have to know where you're currently vibrating. What is your current frequency? Understanding your current frequency is the foundation for personal growth and positive change.

Just as if you were planning a trip, you have to know your starting point before you can map out the path to your destination. This assessment will help you identify your overall frequency vibration, whether it tends to lean toward negative or positive vibrations.

When you're finished with the test, you'll know exactly where you *currently* stand. For this assessment to work, you'll need to be authentic and brutally honest with yourself. There are no "right" or "wrong" answers, only insights that will help you understand where you are now.

---

[6] Lisa A. Koosis, "The Science of Affirmations: The Brain's Response to Positive Thinking," *MentalHealth.com*, June 25, 2024, https://www.mentalhealth.com/tools/science-of-affirmations

Before you start, grab a notebook to keep track of your answers. Throughout this book, I'll ask you to come back, retake this test, and record your progress. I'm curious to see how much you can raise your frequency by the end of the book. Aren't you?

This self-assessment has two parts. Part 1 is a set of ten questions that help determine your daily frequency patterns. You'll rate each answer on a scale of 1 to 10, with 1 being extremely negative and 10 being extremely positive.

Part 2 is a set of five multiple-choice questions based on behavioral indicators. You'll choose the answer that best describes your *typical* behavior.

A scoring guide is provided at the end of the test, along with an interpretation of your score to determine your current frequency levels or vibrational areas.

My Vibrational Frequency: A Self-Assessment Test

Part 1: Daily Frequency Patterns

Rate each question on a scale of 1 to 10:

- 1–3: Extremely Negative / Very Negative
- 4–5: Slightly Negative / Neutral
- 6–7: Slightly to Moderately Positive
- 8–10: Very Positive / Extremely Positive

Questions:

1. How do you typically feel when you first wake up in the morning? Consider your immediate emotional state before external factors influence your day.
2. What thoughts predominantly occupy your mind throughout the day? Think about the general tone and nature of your recurring thoughts.
3. How would you rate the overall positivity of the five people you spend the most time with? Consider their general outlook, energy, and influence on your mood.
4. How do you feel about your everyday work, job, or main daily activities? Rate your overall satisfaction and attitude toward your primary responsibilities.
5. What are your predominant thoughts about the people in your professional and daily life? Consider your general perspective on colleagues, clients, or people with whom you regularly interact.
6. How do you feel about your relationship with your partner, spouse, or closest relationship? If single, consider your overall satisfaction with your relationship status.
7. How do you perceive people typically respond to you? Consider both friends and strangers. Do they seem drawn to you or put off by your energy?
8. When encountering stressful situations or difficult people, how do you typically respond? Rate based on whether your response tends to be constructive or destructive.

9. When someone is inconsiderate, like cutting you off in traffic, how do you typically respond? Consider both your immediate reaction and how long it affects your mood.
10. What are your predominant thoughts at the end of each day before you go to bed? Think about whether you tend to reflect positively or dwell on problems.

Part 2: Behavioral Indicators

Choose the answer that best describes your typical behavior.

11. When you first wake up in the morning, you're most likely to:
    » Turn on the news or check negative headlines.
    » Listen to music, podcasts, or audiobooks.
    » Exercise, meditate, do yoga, or journal.
    » Check or scroll through social media.

12. Which statement best describes your dominant thought patterns and approach to life?
    » I regularly experience thoughts of gratitude and focus on positive aspects.
    » I often find myself dwelling on resentments and negative experiences.
    » I feel aligned with my purpose and intentional about my path.
    » I feel stuck, directionless, or like I'm just going through the motions.

13. When faced with a challenge or setback, you typically:
    » Look for lessons learned and opportunities for growth.
    » Focus on what went wrong and who's to blame.
    » Seek solutions and take action to improve the situation.

» Feel overwhelmed and avoid dealing with it.
14. In conversations, you tend to:
    » Share positive experiences and encourage others.
    » Vent about problems and discuss what's wrong with the world.
    » Listen actively and offer constructive support.
    » Stay surface level to avoid deeper connections.
15. When you think about your future, you generally feel:
    » Excited and optimistic about the possibilities.
    » Worried and pessimistic about potential problems.
    » Motivated and purposeful about your goals.
    » Uncertain and anxious about what lies ahead.

Scoring Guide

Part 1 Scoring (Questions 1–10)

- Add up your ratings for all 10 questions
- Total possible: 100 points

Part 2 Scoring (Questions 11–15)

For each question, assign points as follows:

- a = 4 points
- b = 1 point
- c = 4 points
- d = 2 points

Total possible: 20 points

Overall Assessment:

Combined Total Score: _____ / 120

How to Interpret Your Frequency Score

Predominantly Positive Mindset (85–120 points)

You generally maintain a positive outlook and constructive approach to life. You likely:

- Wake up with energy and optimism.
- Focus on solutions rather than problems.
- Surround yourself with positive influences.
- Handle stress with resilience, ease, or efficiency.
- End your days with gratitude and reflection.

Frequency Boost: Continue strengthening your positive practices while being mindful not to suppress authentic emotions when processing difficulties.

Mixed/Transitional Mindset (60–84 points)

You show a blend of positive and negative patterns. You likely:

- Have good days and challenging days with varying outlooks.
- Recognize both opportunities and obstacles.
- Might be in a period of growth or transition.
- Have some positive influences, but also some draining relationships or situations.

Frequency Boost: Focus on identifying your strongest positive patterns and expanding them while gradually addressing the negative patterns that hold you back, reducing or eliminating them altogether when possible.

Predominantly Negative Mindset (35–59 points)

You lean toward negative thought patterns and may struggle with pessimistic outlooks. You likely:

- Start days feeling heavily overwhelmed, or dreading what's ahead.
- Focus on problems, limitations, and what's wrong.
- May be surrounded by negative influences or feel isolated.
- Handle stress by avoiding or blaming other people or circumstances.
- End days dwelling on difficulties or disappointments.

Frequency Boost: Begin with small, manageable changes to your daily routine and thought patterns. Consider seeking support through counseling, positive communities, or personal development resources. Additionally, walking or other exercise can increase dopamine and help you clear your mind.

Significantly Negative Mindset (Below 35 points)

Your current mindset patterns may be significantly impacting your well-being and satisfaction with life. Consider reaching out to a mental health professional, counselor, or trusted friend for support. You deserve to feel better, and help is available in many different forms.

You Can Change Your Frequency Starting Now!

Regardless of your current frequency score, you can change your beliefs. Your mindset is not permanently fixed. It can be developed and improved when you start believing in a future that holds everything you want in life.

That's why you picked up this book, right? You believe there is a better future for you. At least, you *hope* there is. And if hope is all you have right now, that's okay, tap into it. I know a guy who can help you with that! By the time you reach the last page, you'll *believe*.

When you commit to completing the assessment in this chapter and to putting the principles taught in this book into practice, you'll see your life change right before your eyes, just like I did.

I didn't write this book to impress you with my stories. I wrote it to activate you. I believe in you and your ability to raise your frequency and design a life that reflects your deepest desires, hopes, and dreams to the fullest extent imaginable.

Small, consistent changes create lasting transformation, but awareness is the first step. You've already begun by taking the My Vibrational Frequency Self-Assessment Test. Consider retaking the assessment every 14 days to track your progress as you implement the practices I'll teach you. And don't forget to be patient and compassionate with yourself. Positive changes and mindset adjustments take time.

In the next chapter, we'll talk about the 12 Universal Laws that govern the universe and how they are the foundation for your success. Understanding and applying these laws is key to aligning your thoughts and actions with your goals and aspirations. Your highest level of health, prosperity, and well-being can be achieved simply by intentionally implementing the universal laws.

CHAPTER 3

The 12 Universal Laws— Your Foundation for Vibrational Success

I first learned about the 12 Universal Laws very early in my network marketing career. The gentleman who introduced me to them suggested that I become familiar with the 12 Universal Laws and apply them in my life and my business.

At first, I resisted. But then I began to see how the 12 Universal Laws were the common denominator in all of the people I saw having tons of success. These high achievers were all actively applying the concepts and principles. I quickly understood that if I wanted to be a high achiever, the 12 Universal Laws were essential to elevate my frequency and achieve extraordinary results.

These 12 laws govern the energetic fabric of our reality and provide the blueprint for conscious creation. When you align your thoughts, emotions, and actions with these principles, you unlock your capacity to manifest your highest potential.

If the 12 Universal Laws Are So Important, Where Did They Come From?

The 12 Universal Laws stem from ancient Hermetic philosophy, a spiritual philosophy about how the universe works.[7] It was popularized by texts like *The Kybalion*, originally published in 1908, which outlined seven principles from the Egyptian and Greek sage Hermes Trismegistus.

Through time, the seven principles were expanded into 12 interconnected laws by New Age thought leaders, combining the spiritual concepts from various traditions like Hawaiian Hoʻoponopono. The result is a set of guiding principles for life and manifestation. Instead of a single inventor, the 12 Universal Laws are seen as observed truths about how reality works, not scientific laws.

You are probably familiar with the Law of Attraction. This law has received the vast majority of the spotlight over the past few decades. You may also have heard of the Law of Vibration and the Law of Cause and Effect, also known as Karma. But all 12 Universal Laws are important as they work together to raise your frequency and shape your reality for greater fulfillment.

In this chapter, I'll provide an overview of each law and how to use it effectively to raise your frequency and vibration, so you can start manifesting everything you want in life. After reading each law, take time to consider how it applies to you because each one does, whether you realize it or not.

---

[7] "The Kybalion: 7 Hermetic Principles Explained in Simple Terms," *Sol Good Media*, Accessed December 15, 2025, https://solgoodmedia.com/blog/the-kybalion-7-hermetic-principles-explained-in-simple-terms.

1. The Law of Divine Oneness

The Law of Universal Oneness is the foundation of all connection. This fundamental law reveals that separation is merely an illusion. There is no "your mind" and "my mind." There is only one universal mind, and every person, animal, plant, rock, and particle in existence is interconnected through this divine matrix of universal energy.

This can be a difficult concept to grasp, but when you do, you realize that every thought you think, every emotion you feel, and every action you take sends ripples throughout the entire cosmic web, and those ripples touch countless others. Some people refer to this as the Divine Source or Spirit, and it is one universal mind that connects us all.

Practice Living This Law

Understanding oneness transforms how you interact with the world around you. Some people can tap into the Divine Source or the Universal Oneness better than others. This just means that they are raising their vibration to a level that they can now recognize or be aware of Universal Oneness. Through dedicated practice of the principles and techniques in this book, you, too, can get better at tapping into that source.

When you operate from a place of unity consciousness, your vibration naturally rises because you're no longer fighting against the flow of universal energy. Empathy becomes your superpower, and compassion becomes your frequency amplifier. Practice seeing yourself in others, having grace, and recognizing that by elevating others, you elevate yourself.

2. The Law of Attraction

Made famous by *The Secret*, a 2006 self-help book and documentary film by Rhonda Byrne, this law demonstrates that your external reality is a *direct reflection* of your internal frequency. Think of this law as the mirror of your inner world. Whatever beliefs and emotions you experience internally, either consciously or unconsciously, are reflected in your outer world or environment.

The Law of Attraction isn't just about positive thinking. Yes, you have to think and act positively to attract positive outcomes. But it also requires deep, authentic belief coupled with aligned emotions. You have to believe *and* feel positive thoughts and emotions that raise your energy and vibration to a level that will attract the positive outcomes you want. Your subconscious programming, emotional patterns, and core beliefs are the true architects of your reality.

This law is important, as they all are, but it's not enough just by itself. What's missing in the Law of Attraction is action, which we'll talk about in the Law of Inspired Action. To demonstrate why you need to take action, consider this example: You're sitting in your living room, and it starts to get warm. You think, "I wish it were cooler." But the temperature isn't going to magically drop ten degrees. You can *think* all the positive thoughts you want about cool breezes and chilled air, but the temperature will not change. You have to go to the thermostat and physically adjust the temperature.

Practice Living This Law

To harness this law effectively, you must align your conscious desires with your subconscious beliefs. This means doing the inner work to clear limiting beliefs and emotional blocks. We'll talk about how to do that more in chapter 8. When your thoughts, feelings, and beliefs vibrate at the same frequency as your desires, manifestation becomes inevitable. Rather than dwelling on what's missing, focus on embodying the feeling of already having what you want.

3. The Law of Vibration

As mentioned previously, everything is energy in motion. That means, at the quantum level, everything in existence is pure energetic vibration at different frequencies. Your thoughts, emotions, and your physical body all vibrate. Even your environment holds a vibrational signature.

Remember, if you wake up in the morning and feel like your life isn't going the way you planned, it's because you're operating at a low vibration. But you can change your vibration. You can raise your frequency. As discussed, low vibrations produce negative results; high vibrations produce positive results. The phrase "like attracts like" isn't just a metaphor. It's simple physics.

Practice Living This Law

Your vibrational frequency is your energetic signature, and it determines what you attract into your life. To raise your frequency, focus on thoughts and activities that generate positive emotions: gratitude, love, joy, excitement, and peace.

Notice how your social circle reflects your current vibration. If you want to change your life, sometimes you need to change your energetic environment and your circle of "friends."

4. The Law of Correspondence

The central tenet of the Law of Correspondence is "as above, so below." You could also say "as within, so without," meaning that your external world serves as a reflection of your internal state. The patterns in your external life reflect the patterns of your internal world. The relationship you have with yourself is reflected in the relationships you have with others. Your financial situation reflects your beliefs about abundance as well. So if you want to change your external world, you must first change your internal world. In this way, you are not just a passive observer of your life, but an active co-creator of your reality.

The Law of Correspondence is about balance. It says there can't be an up without a down, a good without a bad, or light without dark. The mistake people often make is focusing too much on the negative, and they forget to look for the inevitable positive. As long as there are negative aspects, there must be a positive aspect. For example, when I say, "I was homeless, living in my car," your mind immediately thinks about the negative connotations of that situation. But when I say, "I was homeless, living in my car, and it was the springboard of my success," you can see both the negative and the positive. There will always be opportunities in your path; you just have to look for and focus on them.

Practice Living This Law

Use this law as a diagnostic tool. Look at the patterns in your life. What keeps repeating? These external patterns point to internal frequencies that need attention. By changing your inner patterns through conscious awareness and intentional practice, you automatically shift the corresponding outer patterns.

5. *The Law of Inspired Action*

The often overlooked Law of Inspired Action is crucial for manifesting. This law is like a bridge between vision and reality. Your intentions and desires (Law of Attraction) must be matched with aligned action (Law of Inspired Action). The universe responds to movement. When you take a step toward your dreams, the universe takes a step toward you, just like a magnet.

The Law of Inspired Action also requires that the action be aligned with your core values and beliefs. That's the "inspired" part. You have to have a purpose and be vigorous in the action you take.

Remember the example of turning up the thermostat? Your desire for cooler temperatures must be matched with the action of changing the temperature on the thermostat. You can't just manifest cooler air; you have to take action.

Practice Living This Law

Inspired action feels different from forced action. It flows from intuition rather than desperation, or from excitement rather than obligation. Others cannot force it upon you. When you vibrate at a high frequency, the actions you're inspired to take will feel energizing and aligned. Trust your inner guidance and take action from a place of joy and anticipation rather than fear and scarcity.

6. *The Law of Cause and Effect (Karma)*

Every action creates a reaction; every cause produces an effect. It's like a boomerang of energy. What you send out into the universe must and will return to you—often in ways you don't expect and through channels you couldn't predict. Karma is often mistaken for a punishment or reward, but it's actually a natural flow of energy responding to high or low frequencies.

When you put negative energy out into your environment, you're going to get negative results. But when you have positive, abundant thoughts, you send the signal that you are open to receiving positive energy and abundance.

Practice Living This Law

As mentioned, the first step is to recognize your current state, and then take inspired action to change it. You can use this law to consciously and purposefully send out positive sparks of high-frequency energy. When you consistently emit high-frequency thoughts, emotions, and actions, you create a positive feedback loop that amplifies your vibrational state. Be mindful of the energy you're putting out, as it will inevitably circle back to you multiplied.

7. The Law of Compensation

While similar to the Law of Cause and Effect, this law focuses specifically on the energy behind your actions. I've always said that the surest way to get anything you want in life is to help others get what they want. If you want positive results, help others get positive results, and then all the things you want will naturally flow to you. Be mindful, though…helping others get what they want cannot be detrimental to your core beliefs.

It's not just what you do, but the vibrational quality of your heart when you do it. The help or service you provide to others has to come from a place of genuine love and care. If you try to fake your emotions, it won't work. The universe reads your energetic intention as well as your physical actions.

Practice Living This Law

Before acting, check your heart and your motivations. When you give from a place of genuine love, speak from authentic truth and serve from sincere compassion; the compensation you receive matches that high-frequency energy. This creates an upward spiral of abundance in all areas of your life.

8. The Law of Perpetual Transmutation of Energy

"Transmutation of energy" sounds kind of scary, doesn't it? Here is the concept: Energy can neither be created nor destroyed, but it is constantly in motion and changing form. Take water, for example. It can be ice, liquid, or steam, but it's always water at its core, just in different states.

Frequencies are not fixed, which is why you can raise yours. You have the power to transmute, or convert, lower vibrational energy into higher vibrational energy through conscious intention and focused attention. The most compelling part of this truth is that higher vibrations, like gratitude, love, and positive thoughts, will always transform lower vibrations like anger, fear, or despair when you consciously direct them. Since frequencies are not fixed, you must work on raising them every day.

For example, you can turn negative emotions like anger or frustration into motivation to take action. You can transform limiting beliefs into abundant, empowering beliefs. It's the same energy; you've just transformed it. You've raised the frequency and vibration.

Practice Living This Law

You can change your vibration at any moment. When you feel stuck in low-frequency emotions or situations, remember that everything is energy in motion. If you're stuck in a negative situation, you have the power to change it by consistently introducing higher-frequency energy through your thoughts, actions, and focus. Using tools like meditation, visualization, breathwork, or music can shift your energy and raise your frequency in real time. It's actually very powerful when you learn how to use it.

9. The Law of Relativity

The universe itself is not good or bad. It's your perception that assigns meaning to experiences. Nothing is inherently good or bad until you compare it to something else. Your mind makes judgments based on comparisons to past experiences. You may think you're having a bad day, but it's only "bad" compared to the "good" day you had last week.

The good news is that you can change your situation at any time. Through understanding the 12 Laws of the Universe and using the tools I'll teach you, you can raise your vibration and start seeing more "good" days, comparatively. You'll always experience ups and downs (The Law of Rhythm). It's how you respond to those shifts and recognize that everything is relative that helps you put each day in perspective.

Practice Living This Law

Take responsibility for the meaning you assign to experiences and respond appropriately. When you view challenges as opportunities for growth and view negative situations with empowering thoughts, you maintain a higher frequency regardless of external circumstances. Practice reframing situations to find the gift or lesson within them. Put on your rose-colored glasses and see the positive in every situation. Trust me, it's always there.

10. *The Law of Gender*

This law isn't about biological gender. It's about the two complementary forces that exist in everything: masculine (yang) and feminine (yin) energies. Masculine energy is action-oriented, focused, and directive; it's the "doing" energy. Feminine energy is receptive, intuitive, and creative. It's the "being" energy of trusting the process, nurturing ideas, and being open to possibilities. We shift into these masculine and feminine energies all the time without giving it a second thought.

These two energies complement each other and create balance not just in humans, but also throughout the universe. You'll find that these two fundamental energies are present in all creation. Balancing and integrating both energies within yourself is the key to harmony, manifestation, and personal growth.

Practice Living This Law

Success requires you to honor both your masculine and feminine energies. Use masculine energy to set clear intentions, take focused action toward your goals, and maintain discipline. Use feminine energy to receive inspiration, trust your intuition and timing, and allow manifestation to unfold. When these energies are balanced, you operate from your highest frequency and greatest power.

11. The Law of Polarity

Everything has an opposite, and these opposites are necessary for growth and appreciation. You couldn't know joy without having experienced sadness; you couldn't appreciate abundance without having known lack. Similar to the Law of Correspondence, the Law of Polarity shows us that people often dwell too much on the negative and forget to look for the positive. Polarity provides the contrast necessary for conscious choice and spiritual evolution.

Polarity suggests opposites, but another way to view it is that two things can be different manifestations of the same thing. Take hot and cold, for instance. They are both degrees of temperature, but they are on opposite ends of the spectrum. The same could be said of light and darkness, which are on different levels of illumination. From these examples, you can see that seemingly opposing elements are interconnected as part of a larger whole, and everything exists in relation to its opposite.

Practice Living This Law

Instead of resisting negative experiences, think of them as one end of the spectrum. What's at the other end? Positive experiences. Then, using the Law of Inspired Action, take steps to move the experience from a negative to a positive. While the change from hot to cold seems to happen instantaneously, there is actually a range of temperature changes that occur along the way.

Negative experiences provide valuable contrast that helps you clarify what you truly want (and what you *don't* want). Use challenging times as launching pads for greater clarity and stronger desires. The deeper you've been in lower frequencies, the higher you can potentially rise. The key is to celebrate each "temperature" change during the process.

12. *The Law of Rhythm*

Everything moves in natural cycles and rhythms. The seasons, tides, economic cycles, emotional cycles, and life phases are all part of an organic rhythm. There are always ups and downs. It's never stagnant. If you find yourself at a low point, don't dwell on it. Soon, the tide will change, and you'll find yourself back on top again as long as you continue to implement the changes necessary for growth.

Understanding these natural rhythms prevents you from becoming attached to any particular state and helps you move with life's ebbs and flows. It's important to accept both the positive and negative experiences as natural parts of life. You want to strive for balance without getting too attached to the highs or the lows.

Practice Living This Law

Work with natural rhythms rather than against them. There are times for expansion and times for contraction; times for action and times for rest. By honoring these cycles and not fighting them, you maintain a more stable, higher frequency overall. Trust that after every low cycle comes a high cycle, and use quiet periods to prepare for your next expansion.

Adopting the 12 Universal Laws Into Your Life

These 12 Universal Laws work together as an integrated ecosystem. They're not separate principles but interconnected components of how energy moves through the universe. As you study and apply these laws, you'll begin to see how they weave together to create the tapestry of your experience.

For example, imagine you set a goal to change your life for the better, whether that's your career, your finances, or your relationships. The moment you set your intention, your energy begins to shift, activating the Law of Vibration. Then, opportunities that match your new mindset begin to come to you. That's the Law of Attraction. As you take each small, inspired step toward your goal, you're putting the Law of Inspired Action into motion, bridging the gap between desire and reality.

Along the way, challenges and setbacks appear, but every obstacle contains an opposite opportunity (Law of Polarity), and every action you take creates a ripple—the Law of Cause and Effect.

Consistent practice and patient observation are the keys to using these laws to raise your frequency. Start by focusing on one or two laws that resonate most strongly with you, then gradually incorporate the others. Remember, mastery comes from practical application in your daily life, not the perfect understanding of how and why it works.

When you align your life with these universal principles, not only will you raise your frequency, but you will also become the higher frequency that uplifts everyone and everything around you. This is the true frequency of success: achieving your personal goals and becoming a force for positive change in the world.

In theory, raising your frequency and vibration is simple, but putting it into daily practice takes effort. You'll encounter resistance along the way, and that's what we'll talk about next. In chapter 4, I'll share the common hurdles you'll face as you work on raising your frequency.

CHAPTER 4

Overcoming Turbulence—Three Obstacles to Watch Out For

I've said it before, but it deserves repeating: Raising your frequency and vibration isn't necessarily easy. Sometimes it is, depending on the situation, but most often it takes consistent, conscious effort. Because try as you might, you will face setbacks and obstacles. Raising your frequency is not always a linear upward path. You will be challenged on every front and will have to find a way to overcome those barriers to success. In this chapter, we're diving deep into three of the most common obstacles you'll face as you embark on your vibration and frequency-raising adventure, and you'll need to be aware of them to achieve success.

One of the biggest challenges comes from your very own subconscious called limiting beliefs. These are the ideas and values that you *think* define you. But they are really false beliefs you picked up from the perceived opinions of others. And they don't serve you well. They keep you from living authentically.

The second obstacle arises from other external factors, such as your environment. Remember in chapter 1 when we talked about the energetic wildcard? Yep, people. The people you surround yourself with can sabotage your efforts. Perhaps you have heard the saying, "If you lie down with dogs, you get up with fleas." Another saying is, "You are the company you keep," meaning, take care to surround yourself with the type of person you aspire to be. The people you surround yourself with can help you raise your frequency—so choose wisely!

The final obstacle we'll talk about is using forgiveness to cope with hurt and resentment. Anger, hurt, and resentment are low-frequency vibrations that will derail any effort to raise your vibration. It's so much easier to live a high-frequency life when you're not burdened with the weight of anger and bitterness. At the end of this chapter, I'll share my personal story about forgiveness, and how it was the miracle I didn't know I needed.

But now, if you're ready, strap in and let's start with limiting beliefs.

Obstacle #1: Limiting Beliefs

At one time, it was considered impossible to run a mile in under four minutes. The experts agreed that if a person were to run a mile in under four minutes, their heart would explode. The four-minute mile was thus deemed an insurmountable human limitation. The record time of 4:01.3 had stood for nine years and was considered to be unbreakable.

Roger Bannister, a young medical student, believed otherwise. On May 6, 1954, he broke the four-minute mile with a time of 3:59.4 while fighting a 15-mile-per-hour crosswind.[8]

Within the next month, three new people broke the four-minute mile, and over the following year, more than 19 people had broken the so-called unbreakable barrier.

Until Bannister achieved this monumental feat, it was considered impossible. But once he shattered the record, many people realized that it really *was* possible. This produced a paradigm shift in the world of running, and the previous limiting belief was shattered.

Thanks to Bannister and those who immediately followed him, the world found out that it was now possible for a human to run a sub-four-minute mile without their heart exploding. The impossible became possible.

Before that momentous day, people were conditioned to believe that this athletic feat was unattainable, but Bannister did not accept this old conditioning and crushed the limiting belief that was held by so many for so long.

Prior to becoming involved in personal development, I held on to some old conditioning and limiting beliefs. I did not believe, nor could I imagine, making $100,000 in a year. But as I began to have success, my belief system changed.

The first time I made $30,000 in one month, I realized I could make $50,000 in a month by raising my belief. Then, as I closed in on my first $50,000 month, I expanded my belief

---

[8] "Roger Bannister Runs First Four-Minute Mile," *History.com*, May 27, 2025, https://www.history.com/this-day-in-history/may-6/first-four-minute-mile.

system again. This time, a $100,000 month no longer seemed impossible; it now felt inevitable.

My old conditioning had me believe that I could not make $100,000 *in an entire year*. My new belief showed me that it was possible to make $100,000 *in a single month*. And I did!

I like to think that Roger Bannister and I have something in common: We both challenged our conditioning and changed our belief system. And so can you.

The key is to recognize that you don't need to know *how* you're going to do it. The first step is to *believe* it is possible. The *how* or the *action* will take care of itself. Just like Bannister believed he could break the four-minute mile and I believed I could make $100,000 in a single month, you have the power to create anything you desire for yourself. It's simply a matter of increasing your level of awareness to become conscious of your new belief.

This was a huge shift in my conditioning and a perfect example of how limiting beliefs work.

Where Do Limiting Beliefs Come From?

If limiting beliefs keep you stuck, where do they come from, and how can you change them? The first step is to believe you *can* change them. Just like Banister did. Just like I did.

The next step is to understand that most limiting beliefs are not yours. You involuntarily adopted them when they were handed to you by your parents, teachers, coworkers, and friends. These limiting beliefs represent your current paradigm.

Since these beliefs didn't come from you, it means that they aren't really a part of you. You don't have to keep holding on to them if you don't want to. You can release them any time you're ready. Of course, that's often easier said than done. Or, once you recognize them, you can use these limiting beliefs as stepping stones to success. When someone says you can't, prove them wrong!

How Can I Change My Limiting Beliefs?

You may have been holding on to some of these beliefs since early childhood. They may be so ingrained in your psyche that they feel like an extension of you, like they are part of your identity. When you strip them away, you'll probably feel uncomfortable at first. And that's okay because it gives you a chance to get curious about what you want and open your mind to new possibilities.

Ask yourself the following questions and then journal about or write out your answers:

- What's something I really want, but feel like I can't have or achieve?
- What thoughts pop up when I imagine going for it?
- Who or what told me I couldn't do it, or that it's not for people like me?
- If I knew success was guaranteed, what would I do differently?

Take time to dig deep and answer these questions as honestly as you can. Limiting beliefs are sneaky; they can disguise themselves as strengths. For instance, you might *think* you prefer sticking to a schedule and a comfortable routine but in reality, you're afraid of failure, so you avoid the challenges that come with stepping out of your comfort zone.

Perhaps you have a limiting belief on being "realistic" or "practical." You might think you're a realistic optimist, but the truth is that you are holding yourself back from your true potential because you're afraid of what people might think if you become super successful.

Once you identify your limiting beliefs, you'll begin to notice how often they come up for you. Many times it shows up in what you say when you talk to yourself: *I'm not good enough, I'm not smart enough, I'm always a loser*. You'll recognize that negative self-talk for what it really is—fear. As you recognize your limiting beliefs, don't be afraid to challenge them. Ask yourself, What is true? And then reflect on the best path forward.

As you shed your limiting beliefs and start living more authentically, your frequency and vibration will naturally increase. It's like the sun breaking through the clouds after a storm. Shedding limiting beliefs will feel as good as soaking up the sun and dancing in the puddles.

Self-Assessment

1. List your top three negative beliefs. Some examples are:
    - » I never have enough time.
    - » I never have enough money.
    - » I'm not talented enough.
    - » I'm too old.
    - » I need to be perfect.
    - » I'm afraid of failure (or success).

2. Now look at your list and ask yourself:
   » Which belief shows up most often in my daily life?
   » Which one seems to feed into the others? For example, "I need to be perfect" might also fuel the fear of failure or not feeling talented enough.
   » Which belief holds me back in more than one area of my life? (Relationships, work, health, finances.)
3. The first limiting belief I will challenge is _____.
4. Every time this limiting belief comes up, I'll flip the script by saying _____.

You don't need to challenge them all at once. Start with the one that feels the strongest. When you shift that belief, the others will often begin to unravel too.

Obstacle #2: External Influences

From the time I was very young, I played sports. Whether it was football, basketball, track, wrestling, hacky sack, or indoor volleyball, I always loved playing with people who were better than me. I liked being around higher-level athletes because they inspired me to be better and to raise my own game. And because I played with better athletes, I naturally increased my skill level. That's the power of your environment.

There's a success principle that says: You become like the people you surround yourself with. So if that's true, and I believe it is, why not surround yourself with the most positive, driven, and successful people you can find?

Environment matters. Relationships matter. And if you're serious about increasing your frequency and achieving meaningful results, you've got to pay attention to both.

Weed Out the Negative People

One of the biggest hurdles you'll face when trying to achieve success is the constant negative influence of those around you.

You'll hear it from every direction:

- "Don't waste your time."
- "That will never work."
- "You're setting yourself up for failure."
- "Be realistic."
- "Why don't you just get a real job?"
- "You shouldn't try something so risky."
- "Those things never work."

The crazy thing is that comments like these often come from the people closest to you, like your friends, family, coworkers, and teachers. They say these things because they care about you and don't want to see you fail, and they think they're protecting you by attempting to dissuade you from even trying.

So, realistically, it's not about you at all—it's about *their* discomfort. Because when you raise your frequency and go after your goals, it reminds them of what they're *not* doing. And that can make them feel small and insignificant. So they try to keep you down because if they can't be successful, why should you be? It's like the classic story about crabs in a bucket.

Crab Mentality

A fisherman picks up a crab and places it in a bucket. The crab starts to climb out, but before it can, the fisherman places another crab inside. Now, when the first crab attempts to climb out of the bucket, the second crab grabs hold of it and pulls it back down.

As each new crab is placed inside with the others, it tries to climb out, but is pulled back down by the group. Thus, no crabs escape, and they are all stuck in the bucket to meet their fate.

This is called crab mentality. It's the idea that when one person tries to rise, others (sometimes unintentionally) hold them back out of doubt, fear, insecurity, envy, or the idea that "If I can't succeed, neither can you." Those who have a scarcity mentality fear that others' success will limit their ability to succeed. The result is that everyone remains stuck, no one escapes the bucket, and no one succeeds.

That's why you have to be intentional with your environment and the people you surround yourself with. You have to start weeding out the negative influences. Obviously, you may not be able to cut *everyone* out, especially family, but you can create boundaries. You can protect your energy by creating exit strategies for situations you know will drain you and bring your frequency down.

Add Positive People to Your Circle

Just like weeds can choke out the flowers in a garden if left unchecked, negativity chokes out growth. But when you surround yourself with positive people who challenge you to be better, everything changes.

It's important to find people who lift you up. People who are going after their goals, who believe that success is inevitable, and who never say, "You can't do that." Surround yourself with people who raise your frequency just by being in the room. Mingling, socializing, and strategizing with people who operate at a higher level than you allows you to tap into that positive frequency and grow right along with them.

And it's important to be that kind of person for others too. The kind of person who lifts others up and cheers them on. Just like baby sea turtles.

Turtle Mentality

As baby sea turtles hatch, they wait in the nest for the rest of the hatchlings to emerge from their shells. Once they have all struggled out of their shells, they coordinate their efforts, digging together to reach the top of the nest. By working as a group, they minimize the effort each turtle needs to expend, making their next adventure—the mad dash to the ocean—easier and less taxing.

Create a Thriving Environment

The concept of surrounding yourself with what you want to become applies to virtually every area of your life. From sports to businesses to relationships and everything in between.

Success, at its core, is simple. But simple doesn't mean easy. It requires work. You have to be relentless in your pursuit of it and willing to see every failure as a stepping stone. To succeed, you need to be crystal clear about what success looks like—and never let anyone else define it for you.

Don't let yourself get pulled back into the bucket with the other crabs. And don't stay buried in the sand. Dig your way out to the surface with people who are rising too. Surround yourself with high-frequency achievers who push you forward and create an environment where growth is the norm and success is expected.

Self-Assessment
1. What "crabs" are holding me back? Crabs can be negative influences, bad habits, limiting beliefs, or toxic environments. Look for anything or anyone that drains your energy or discourages you.
2. Who are the "turtles" in my life? Turtles are the positive influences. They lift you up, inspire you, and model the success mindset you want to achieve.
3. How can I be like a turtle instead of a crab? Hint: celebrate wins, support others, surround yourself with high-frequency people.

Obstacle #3: Hurt and Resentment

Imagine walking through your career and personal life while carrying hundreds of pounds of bricks on your back. Every meeting you attend, every relationship you build, every opportunity you pursue—all while bearing this crushing weight.

This is precisely what happens when you carry resentment and anger through your daily life. These low-frequency vibrations don't just affect your emotional state; they fundamentally limit your capacity to achieve all that you desire.

When you harbor resentment, your mental and emotional resources become tied up in a constant loop of negative thinking. Your mind, which should be free to innovate, strategize, and recognize opportunities, becomes consumed with replaying past hurts and imagining future confrontations. This mental static interferes with your ability to think clearly, make sound decisions, and maintain the focus necessary for high-level performance.

The Science of Forgiveness

Neuroscience research shows that persistent anger and resentment trigger a sustained release of stress hormones, like cortisol. This impairs memory, reduces creativity, and weakens your immune system. When you operate in a depleted state, shrouded in negativity, you simply cannot perform at your peak. And it shows up in every area of your life from personal relationships and professional networking to cognitive and problem-solving abilities.

Resentment creates a kind of emotional tunnel vision. You become so focused on past wrongs that you miss opportunities all around you. That potential promotion passes you by, the creative juices stop flowing, and friends fall by the wayside—all casualties of carrying those invisible bricks.

The Frequency of Forgiveness

Forgiveness operates on an entirely different vibrational level. When you choose to forgive, you literally free up the negative energy that was trapped in resentment and holding you down. I'm not talking about excusing harmful behavior or pretending that the wrongs didn't occur. I'm not taking accountability out of the equation. True forgiveness is a strategic decision you can make to reclaim your power and redirect your energy toward what you want to *create* (positive) rather than what resentment destroys (negative).

This principle comes intuitively to high achievers. They recognize that every moment spent in resentment is a moment not spent building their vision. They put down the bricks not because they're weak, but because they're smart enough to know that success requires all their available energy and attention.

We have all faced situations where others have wronged us. I want to encourage you to find those instances and consider extending forgiveness. However, I don't think it's fair for me to ask you to forgive without sharing my personal story of living with anger and resentment and the weight that was lifted when I forgave the wrongdoings.

My Miracle of Forgiveness

There's a lot to unpack, and I wish I could tell you a different story. One about growing up with a silver spoon, with parents who shared a beautiful, loving relationship, in a house with a white picket fence. I wish I could say I never lacked for anything and that my parents gave me everything I needed to achieve my dreams. But that is nowhere near my story.

Both of my parents were alcoholics. When I was in first grade, they divorced and my sister and I were sent to a county run "receiving home." It was a place for kids with no parents or parents who couldn't provide proper care. We endured countless custody battles, bouncing between Mom and Dad as they fought in court, each claiming to be the more fit parent. The truth was, neither was truly fit for raising two children.

My mother's alcoholism was severe. She transformed into an amazing woman when she wasn't drinking, but that was rare. At five feet tall and 105 pounds, it didn't take much alcohol to render her completely helpless. I remember walking into her bedroom when I was 10 or 11. She had fallen off the wagon again, and we knew to watch her closely or she'd sneak out for more beer. I found her sitting on the floor in front of her closet, having fallen while checking her hiding places for stashed liquor.

Looking up at me, she said, "I need you to go to the store and buy me some beer."

"Mom, I can't drive, and I can't buy beer. I'm only 10 years old."

"But I need it to get well! Please?"

She continued begging as I told her what I'd said many times before: "Mom, if you don't stop, you're going to kill yourself."

Six months later, I came home from school to find her drunk on the living room floor. My stepdad explained that she'd been in a car accident after drinking and driving. At the hospital, the doctor told her that if she didn't quit drinking, she had about six months to live.

At that moment, I made a decision: I didn't want to watch her die. I told her, my stepdad, and my sister that I was going to live with Dad. I didn't wait for an answer. I called my father and said, "I'm coming to live with you."

My sister, only a year older, chose to stay with Mom. The next day, I was on a plane by myself.

Dad's alcoholism was different. He was a "functioning" alcoholic. At six feet tall and over 200 pounds, alcohol didn't affect him like it did my mother. But that didn't make him any more fit to be a parent. I loved both my parents deeply, but Dad never seemed to put my sister and me first.

As an air traffic controller working crazy shift hours, he was rarely home. When he wasn't working, he'd be at a bar with his drinking buddies until closing time. It wasn't unusual for me not to see him for days. He'd leave for work before I woke up, or I'd be at school before he got up, and I'd be asleep when he came home.

I never had a babysitter. I cooked my own meals and did my own laundry—not bad for a kid who wasn't even a teenager yet. Dad ruled with an iron fist: "Do it my way or get out!" As long as I kept the chores done and dishes clean, life wasn't that bad.

We got the call 18 months after I left Mom and my sister. Dad came into my room one Saturday morning and said, "I got a call this morning." I knew before he spoke. I could see it in his face.

"Your mother died last night."

The only surprise was that she'd lived as long as she had. I didn't even cry. It wasn't that I wasn't sad—it hurt me deeply—but I'd been preparing for this moment for 18 months. At 13, I no longer had a mother. I was a pallbearer at her funeral and still didn't cry. The tears didn't come for over two years, but when they did, they rained and rained.

My father was also a pilot, inspiring my love of aviation. I remember flying in his Cessna 310 when I was 5 or 6, completely consumed with airplanes and flying. He'd take me to the control tower during his midnight shifts, and I became obsessed with aviation. Dad planned for me to begin flying lessons at 14, fly solo at 16, and get my license at 17.

But fate had other plans. In 1981, the air traffic controllers went on strike. Dad had told me it was coming, but not to worry. "There's no way they can fire us all." I supported his decision completely, even walking the picket line with him as a high school freshman.

President Reagan immediately fired 11,000 controllers.

Just like that, my life changed forever. Fortunately, I'd been receiving Social Security checks since Mom's death and had accumulated several thousand dollars. Every couple of weeks, Dad would come to me and say, "I'm going to need to borrow some money, but I promise I'll get it back to you." As if I'd ever say no. I knew he was doing his best to take care of me.

Unfortunately, though, he went three years without steady work. When I was a senior in high school, he and his girlfriend planned to buy a restaurant in a nearby small town. I didn't know it then, but my grandfather had left my sister and me $10,000 each for college. To buy and open the restaurant, Dad used the rest of my account money plus our $20,000 inheritance. He never asked. I didn't even know about the college money until my sister told me Dad had spent it. As a teenager whose next step was college, that money would have made a huge difference for me.

This is where my need for forgiveness began. I "loaned" my father over $15,000 that I never got back.

After college, I worked as a skydive pilot, building flight time for a real flying job. I drove a $500 junker from a "buy here, pay here" lot and slept on Dad's couch—all I could afford. Making less than $1,000 per month flying skydivers, I drove forty miles each way to work.

One day, driving on I-70 in Kansas City, my junker's motor blew up. Dad towed me home and asked, "What are you going to do now?"

"I have no idea."

Knowing I had no money for another car, Dad said, "I'll get $3,000 off my credit card, and you can find something to get you to work." The catch: I had to promise to make the payments. Of course, I agreed. The problem was, I wasn't making enough to support myself and pay the credit card bill, so even though I had the car, I wasn't able to send money to Dad.

The last time Dad and I really spoke, he told me he'd found a place in Minnesota where he could fish and hunt—what he'd always loved. He'd met a widowed woman who owned property she couldn't maintain due to health issues. She offered him rent-free living in exchange for taking care of the place and daily chores.

I helped Dad pack and move to Minnesota. As we got him settled, I hugged him, wished him well, and we said goodbye. That was the last time I saw my father as I knew him.

Soon after returning to Missouri, I took a flight instructor job in Oklahoma. The skydiving season was ending, and I needed work. Shortly after arriving, Dad wrote several letters about the overdue credit card bill, wanting to know when I'd pay it. Even as a flight instructor, I still wasn't making enough to support myself. I told him I couldn't pay due to my low income.

This quickly turned into a written, anger-filled shouting match. I couldn't take it anymore and wrote my final response: "What about all the money you owe me? Where is all that money?"

That was our last communication for over a year and a half.

Fast forward 18 months. I was working for an aircraft charter company in Texarkana, Arkansas—my first "real" flying job. I'd worked extremely hard to reach this point and was excited to finally see my career taking off. At a whopping $816 per month, I was at least moving in the right direction, not financially, but towards my goal of becoming a corporate jet captain.

After returning from a charter flight, I walked into the office to turn in paperwork. The dispatcher handed me a trip packet. "Here's your trip for tomorrow."

"Where am I going?"

"You'll be taking one passenger to Columbia, Missouri, sitting for three hours, then bringing them back."

I was shocked and excited simultaneously. Nobody goes to Columbia, Missouri. Except for the University of Missouri, there's not much there. But I was excited because my sister lived there, and I hadn't seen her since college graduation.

My sister agreed to pick me up at the airport. The next day, I landed on schedule, and she was waiting. At a nearby café, as we caught up on everything since graduate school, she hit me with something I never saw coming.

"I think I should tell you that Dad is here."

My jaw hit the floor. Last I knew, I'd moved him to Minnesota for fishing and hunting. Already knowing about our 18-month silence and why (money), she delivered the next blow. "I have to tell you that he's not doing very well. He's in the VA Hospital. He has cancer again."

I almost fell out of my chair. Questions flooded my mind, but no words came. The arrangement in Minnesota hadn't worked out, and he'd been forced to move. He'd asked my sister for help finding a place and moving. While helping him settle near her in Columbia, he'd asked her to look at a spot on his ribs that concerned him. My sister, a nurse, immediately suggested he see a doctor. Having already battled throat cancer, she knew he was at risk.

After lunch, she dropped me off at the airport. During the return flight to Texarkana, my mind flooded with emotions spanning the entire spectrum. Upon arrival, I immediately requested two days off, explaining that my father was hospitalized and not doing well.

I jumped in my car for the eight-hour drive to Columbia, arriving almost at midnight. I grabbed a hotel room, planning to be at the hospital first thing in the morning.

I arrived at the VA when visiting hours opened. My thoughts consumed me. Would we argue? Would we fight about money? Was he still angry? Would he demand the $3,000? Or would we pretend nothing happened?

At his hospital room door, I froze, terrified of what I'd see. I slowly reached out, turned the knob, and pushed the door open.

Nothing could have prepared me for what I saw. I was shocked. *That can't be my father*, I thought. I didn't recognize him. My 200-pound father had been depleted to what looked like a 90-pound skeleton wrapped in saggy skin. I burst into tears.

He couldn't speak. Most of his motor skills had been destroyed by cancer. The lump on his rib had metastasized to his brain. Once the cancer reached his brain, everything went downhill quickly.

Suddenly, nothing mattered. Not the money. Not the fights. Not the angry words or who owed whom what. It was all erased.

Sobbing in front of my dad, all I could get out was, "I'm sorry! I'm sorry! I'm sorry!"

Though he couldn't speak, tears rolled down his cheeks. We cried and cried. I apologized and, without thinking, took responsibility for everything. "I love you, Dad, and I'm so sorry."

I spent the entire day with him, telling him about my flying adventures, all the places I'd been, all the airplanes I'd flown. Even without words, I could tell he was proud of me. We laughed and cried until visiting hours ended. I kissed his forehead and promised to see him in the morning before returning to work.

The next morning, I spent another couple of hours with him. Again, I told him how sorry I was and that I loved him. We both cried. I kissed him one last time, and then it was time to go.

My mind was so consumed with the emotions and thoughts of the past 48 hours that I couldn't even remember the drive back to Texarkana. I hadn't been home for 24 hours when my sister called.

"Dad passed away this morning."

We buried my father a few days later.

Within minutes of my sister's call, I realized the true, undeniable miracle I'd just experienced. I hadn't spoken to my father in over 18 months. I had no idea what was happening in his life. Nobody goes to Columbia, Missouri. Over 15 pilots on staff could have been assigned that trip, yet 48 hours before my father passed away, I was fortunate enough to be the one to get the trip.

This alone was like finding a needle in a haystack, but combined with the timing—just hours before he died—I call that a miracle. I got to see him, and we were able to let go of all the baggage we'd both been carrying. We both put down the bricks.

I'm not sure how I could have coped without that opportunity. I wouldn't want him burdened with those bricks as he lives his afterlife in heaven.

I don't know if I'll ever experience another miracle as profound as the one I experienced with my father. Even if I'm never graced with another, this one was big enough for a lifetime.

The Freedom to Unload the Bricks

A few years later, I attended a personal development conference in Phoenix. Given the opportunity to speak on an impactful topic, I chose "Forgiveness." In preparation, I recounted my experience with my father and chose to write him a letter.

In that letter, I told him how much I loved him and appreciated our time together before he passed. But what I spent most of my time discussing was forgiveness. I told him I forgave him for all the times he wasn't there for me, for all the times he was sitting in a bar with buddies rather than taking me to school functions, for all the activities I missed because he was too busy, for being late to my high school graduation, and for making me feel like I wasn't enough. And last, for the money.

When I finished, the letter was five pages long. Apparently, I'd still been carrying a few bricks.

I took that letter to the event and walked to the front of the auditorium. Standing squarely in front of the microphone, looking out at a few hundred people, I began to read. By the time I was finished, I don't think there was a dry eye in the room, including mine.

But I was finally brick-free.

The thing about forgiveness is that it doesn't change the past. You can't undo what was done. But forgiveness can change your future.

By unloading the bricks I was carrying, I allowed myself to step into a new and higher frequency. Now, the energy I was using to carry all of that pent-up pain was available for something new—for healing and growth.

That's what forgiveness does. It's an energy shift. It lets you move forward instead of continually living in the past. It breaks the resentment loop. Letting go isn't easy. Sometimes it takes a five-page letter and a flood of tears. But when you finally put the bricks down, you free up energy to raise your frequency and to realize the success that's been waiting for you all along.

Self-Assessment

Take a moment to think about any grudges or resentments that you've been holding on to. Pay attention to the situations or people you replay in your mind—the unresolved conflicts that drain your energy. These are the areas where forgiveness can free your energy and raise your frequency.

1. What hurt or resentment am I holding on to?
2. Who can I forgive?
3. How can I be better to others?

CHAPTER 5

The Four Foundational Pre-FLIGHT Practices

Before you can realize the benefits of high-frequency and high-vibrational living, you need to lay a solid foundation. You can't raise your vibration if your mindset is wobbly or your core habits are nonexistent. Whether you achieve or fail at your goals comes down to applying four foundational practices: tenacity, discipline, consistency, and goals. Do each of these things consistently, and your goals will start becoming your reality faster than you ever thought possible.

Think of this chapter as your pre-flight checklist. These four essential practices will prepare your energy and focus for takeoff. They are non-negotiable, so let's get comfortable with them.

Practice 1: Tenacity

On October 29, 1941, amid the grim days of World War II, Winston Churchill stood behind a podium to address the students at Harrow School in London.

During his notable speech, he spoke the words:

Never give in, never give in, never, never, never, never—in nothing, great or small, large or petty—never give in except to convictions of honour and good sense.[9]

His words provided motivation and a call to resilience during a time of great turmoil, and those words are just as true today as they were then.

There will be times when you think you can't keep going, when fear and doubt cloud your mind, when obstacles crop up like a thunderstorm in your flight plan. But the only way to get what you want is to keep going, even if you have to make a detour or two. To be successful, you must never give in.

History is filled with people who kept showing up, even when it was hard, even when no one believed they could do what they set out to do.

Michael Jordan was cut from his high school varsity basketball team before he went on to become a six-time NBA Champion. His list of accomplishments is inspiring.[10]

Albert Einstein struggled in school, failed his entrance exam for the Swiss Federal Polytechnic School, and faced unemployment and financial hardships.[11] Today, he is

---

9 "Never Give in, Never, Never, Never, 1941." America's National Churchill Museum | Never Give In, Never, Never, Never. Accessed January 7, 2026. https://www.nationalchurchillmuseum.org/never-give-in-never-never-never.html.

10 Elephant Learning, "Michael Jordan: Cut from High School Team, Became an NBA Superstar," *Elephant Learning*, August 27, 2024, https://www.elephantlearning.com/post/michael-jordan-cut-from-high-school-team-became-nba-superstar.

11 Elephant Learning, "Albert Einstein: Overcame Early School Challenges, Won Nobel Prize," *Elephant Learning*, August 27, 2024, https://www.elephantlearning.com/post/albert-einstein-overcame-school-challenges-won-nobel-prize.

renowned for his contributions to the theories of relativity that changed our understanding of space, time, gravity, and the universe.

Sylvester Stallone faced financial hardship and homelessness, living in the New Jersey Port Authority bus station for three weeks. While writing the script for *Rocky*, his electricity was turned off, and he was forced to sell his dog for $25 to get the lights back on. He was rejected by talent agencies over 1,500 times![12] His story is not only one of challenges and setbacks, but also one of resilience and success. The 1976 film, *Rocky*, became a box office hit and earned multiple Academy Awards. He followed that success up with the *Rambo* series, further solidifying his name in Hollywood. And yes, he was able to buy his dog back.[13]

The lesson learned from these stories is that those who keep showing up, keep trying, and failing are the ones who succeed.

Winston Churchill also said, "Success consists of going from failure to failure without the loss of enthusiasm."[14] You must have the courage to keep showing up. If you quit, you are sure to fail, but if you keep going, you are sure to succeed.

---

12 Barnes, Harrison. "Frustration, Rejection, Sylvester Stallone, and Rocky." Harrisonbarnes.com, February 17, 2023. https://www.harrisonbarnes.com/frustration-rejection-sylvester-stallone-and-rocky/#:~:text=As%20he%20tried%20to%20advance,even%20after%20being%20thrown%20out.

13 Tom Ward, "The Amazing Story of the Making of 'Rocky,'" *Forbes*, September 12, 2023, https://www.forbes.com/sites/tomward/2017/08/29/the-amazing-story-of-the-making-of-rocky/

14 A Quote by Winston Churchill," *Goodreads*, accessed December 10, 2025, https://www.goodreads.com/quotes/7697082-success-consists-of-going-from-failure-to-failure-without-loss

Practice 2: Disciplined Action

Nothing will stall your progress faster than taking your eyes off your goals. To achieve success, you'll need to have self-discipline like you've never had before. This isn't the time to be inattentive and disorganized. Your goals and the daily actions you take toward them should be your constant companions.

I'm not saying you have to become like a robot, regimented to the extreme. But you can't half-ass something and expect to get results. Success requires constant attention and nurturing. The success frequency responds to the rhythm and repetition of the consistent, positive energy and vibrations you send out.

Think of discipline as devotion to your future self. The daily habits you perform may not be fun and exciting. They're often simple, a bit boring, and repetitive. But you do them because they align the person you are now with who you are becoming. Self-discipline is the key to your future freedom and success.

Being disciplined is similar to owning a gym membership. Just holding the membership card doesn't change anything for you (except for maybe depleting your bank account). You might be more inclined to go to the gym when you see your membership card sitting on the counter. It can act as a visual connection to your goals. But you have to actually go to the gym and do the work for change to occur.

Also, sporadically going to the gym and doing random workouts won't get you ripped abs or tank top-worthy biceps. It doesn't work like that. It takes discipline to show up and work out consistently, eat nutritiously, and perform all of the other small habits that result in a healthy, toned physique, including something as simple as drinking plenty of water.

So, how can you become more disciplined? You have to know what your goals are, keep them where you can see them, and take action every day. As you work toward increasing self-discipline, try these tips:

1. Start small. Pick one habit to work on at a time.
2. Pair a new habit with a positive habit you already have fully formed.
3. Write your goals down and tape them to your bathroom mirror.
4. Take time to read and review your goals every morning and night.
5. Create positive affirmations to help you stay aligned with your dreams.

Motivation will only get you so far. When the newness wears off and motivation fades, discipline and consistency are the fuel that feeds the fire. That means applying yourself every day, just like taking a shower or brushing your teeth.

Practice 3: Consistent Effort

Self-discipline and consistent effort are two sides of the same coin. You need to practice both if you want to succeed in raising your frequency and vibration.

Simply knowing about the 12 Laws I talked about in chapter 3 doesn't raise your frequency, and thinking about abundance doesn't change your bank account. Applying the laws and acting in alignment with abundance does. But the real key is consistency.

The consistent repetition is what makes it work. You don't have to be perfect, but you do have to keep showing up with intention and continuously putting in the effort.

Michael Jordan and Kobe Bryant are exceptional basketball players. But do you know who has the highest career free-throw percentage in the NBA? Stephen Curry, at 91.1%. Michael Jordan (83.5%) and Kobe Bryant (83.7%) don't even make the top 25 list.[15] So, how did Stephen Curry make such a high percentage of free throws? Practice and repetition.

Stephen dedicated countless hours to practicing and refining his free-throw shooting technique. All of this practice built muscle memory, allowing him to flawlessly execute his free-throw routine, even when the pressure was high.

That's what consistent effort can do for you. It gives you the muscle memory, the confidence, and the mental fortitude to take your shot when the opportunity arises.

Stephen didn't start out on top. During his 2009–2010 rookie season, his free-throw percentage was 88.5%. And throughout his career, it's gone up and down. But he kept applying the principle of consistency, and it paid off.

Oh, and by the way, Stephen Curry also owns the title for most career three-pointers. The lesson here is that when you raise

---

15 "Who Has the Highest Career Free Throw Percentage," *StatMuse*, accessed December 10, 2025, https://www.statmuse.com/nba/ask/who-has-the-highest-career-free-throw-percentage.

your frequency in one area of your life, you'll also raise your frequency in other areas.

The principle of consistency is available to everyone. You don't have to be an NBA player; you just need a goal you want to achieve.

Again, like going to the gym, you won't get into shape with just one visit. It takes dedication and consistently going day after day, using progressive overload to build muscle, and practicing all of the good habits that create a healthy body. Little by little, you obtain the strength and physique you're striving for. And little by little, you achieve the goals you set for yourself.

Practice 4: SMART *Goals*

Goals are like tuning forks for your frequency and vibration. When you set a vague goal, you're essentially trying to play a symphony with an out-of-tune instrument. The result is discordant energy that scatters your focus and diminishes your results. But when you create SMART goals, you fine-tune your intentions to resonate at the exact frequency of success.

SMART goals follow a simple method of creating Specific, Measurable, Achievable, Relevant, and Time-based goals that transform wishful thinking into magnetic attraction. Every element of SMART goals serves to amplify your success frequency and create coherent energy patterns that the universe can respond to. Essentially, setting SMART goals is like turning on a powerful magnet that attracts all the good stuff you want in life.

How does it work? Is it really as simple as setting a few goals and then standing back to watch as they all come to fruition? Well, it's not quite that simple. Here's the thing: Your brain operates on specific frequencies, and so does everything around you. When your goals are fuzzy and not fully formed, your mental frequency is filled with static. It's like a radio trying to pick up every station at once. SMART goals act as your frequency tuner, helping you dial into the exact channel of your desired outcome.

Let's break it down.

S is for Specific: Laser-Focused Vibration

Specificity creates concentrated energy. When you say, "I *want* to be successful," you're broadcasting on a frequency that is so broad it gets lost in the atmosphere. When you say, "I *will* increase my business revenue by 40% through launching two new product lines," you're transmitting a clear, focused signal that the astronauts could probably pick up on the moon.

Specific goals create what quantum physicists call "Quantum Coherence"—all of your mental and emotional resources align toward a single, well-defined, and synchronized outcome. This coherence boosts your power to attract your desired result.

Let's practice:

How would you transform this vague goal into a specific one?

- I want to be healthier.

That goal is ambiguous and indistinct. Instead, a specific health goal could be:

- I will lose 20 pounds to feel healthier and stronger.

Simply saying you'll lose 20 pounds may seem like a vague goal as well, but we'll dial it in with the rest of the SMART goal framework.

Frequency hack:

When writing specific goals, use sensory language. Don't just write what you want; describe how it will look, sound, feel, and even smell. This engages multiple neural pathways and creates higher vibrations.

M is for Measurable: Quantifying Your Success Frequency

The adage, "What gets measured gets managed," is true, but I'll add a second part to that. What gets managed gets magnetized. Measurable goals create feedback loops that keep you vibrationally aligned with your desired outcome.

Numbers carry their own frequency, and when you attach specific metrics to your goals, you essentially give the universe a precise address for delivery. It's the difference between saying "somewhere in Texas" versus providing an exact GPS coordinate.

Let's practice:

How do you measure goals? Every goal needs three types of measurements:

1. Outcome metrics: The final result you want.
2. Process metrics: The activities that lead to the outcome.
3. Leading indicators: Early signals that you're on track.

Using our weight loss example, the measurements would look like this:

- Outcome: Lose 20 pounds and feel healthier and stronger.
- Process: Intermittent fasting and reducing sugar intake.
- Leading Indicators: Clothes feel looser. Energy is better.

Frequency hack:

Create a "Success Dashboard," commonly known as a habit tracker, where you keep track of your metrics either daily (preferred), weekly, or monthly, depending on whether the goal is short-term or long-term. This consistent act of measuring serves as a reminder of what you're working toward and creates a vibrational connection to your goals.

A is for Achievable: Stretching Without Snapping

A common misconception is that "achievable" means "easy." But just because a goal is achievable does not mean it will be easy; it just means that it is possible. Your goals should stretch you beyond your comfort zone without breaking your belief system. When you set goals that are too far out of reach or that feel insurmountable, you naturally create a resistance frequency that actually repels success.

Achievable goals create what I call "confident expectation." It's a high-frequency emotional state that magnetizes opportunities and draws them to you. Goals that feel impossible create doubt and fear, which are low-frequency emotions that repel success and may attract more obstacles instead.

Let's practice:

I have a simple formula for creating an achievable goal. It's called the Stretch Formula, and it works like this: Your goal should be at least 10% beyond what you think you can do, but not so far that you can't visualize the path. This creates optimal tension. It's enough to challenge you and stimulate growth, but not so much that you short-circuit your belief and give up before you've even started.

To see if your goal meets the Stretch Formula criteria, ask yourself these questions:

- Do I have access to the resources I need? Resources may include time, money, skills, or connections.
- Have others achieved similar results under similar circumstances?
- Who in my field or industry has achieved similar success that I can emulate?
- Can I break this down into smaller, more manageable steps?

Going back to the weight loss example, you would first determine if losing 20 pounds would stretch you enough without feeling overwhelmed or if that is too much. You might decide 20 pounds is the perfect amount, or you might feel that losing 10 pounds is more achievable.

Once you decide the number of pounds that feels right for you, you'll think about the resources you may need to help you lose the weight. Do you need a gym membership? Or do you feel comfortable exercising at home to YouTube videos?

Next, look for three people who have achieved the same weight loss goal. On days you struggle, you can look to those people to find the motivation to keep going.

Finally, whether you want to lose 10 pounds or 20, think about how you can break it down into smaller increments. Generally, losing one to two pounds per week is considered safe and doable.

Frequency hack:

For every major goal you make, identify three people who have achieved something similar. Study their path and adopt their strategies. This creates an "achievement frequency" in your subconscious mind. Knowing that someone else has already achieved what you want lets you know that it is possible. Remember Roger Bannister? Once he achieved a sub-four-minute mile, several others followed his lead because they believed this "unbreakable barrier" was now possible. Keep in mind, if no one has achieved the goal that you have set, that does NOT mean you can't achieve it. It will simply require more focused intent on your part.

R is for Relevant: Aligning with Your Core Frequency

Relevant goals resonate with your deepest values and authentic desires. When your goals align with who you really are, you tap into your natural frequency—the vibration at which you operate most powerfully. It's specific to you!

Irrelevant goals create internal conflict. It's like an internal tug-of-war; part of you wants to achieve them, but the other part resists because they don't align with your core self. This internal friction creates chaotic energy that sabotages your efforts.

Let's practice:

To find out if your goal is relevant, ask yourself:

1. Does this goal align with my core values?
2. Will achieving this goal move me closer to my vision of my ideal life?
3. Am I pursuing this for myself or to meet someone else's expectations?
4. Does thinking about this goal energize me or drain me?

As you answer those questions, pay attention to your body's response. Notice what happens physically and emotionally. If the goal is relevant, you will feel expansive and aligned, your breathing deepens, and your chest opens. You feel energized and excited.

If the goal is irrelevant, you'll feel the opposite. You'll feel "off." A sense of heaviness will pervade, and you'll feel tension in your chest or shoulders. Your breathing might become shallow, and you'll have an overall sense of feeling smaller.

To find out if your goal of losing weight is relevant, you would ask:

- Does losing weight align with my core values of becoming healthy and fit?
- Will losing weight move me closer to my ideal life?
- Do I want to lose weight for myself? Or am I feeling pressure from others?

- Does thinking about losing weight excite me? Or make me feel worse about myself?

Frequency hack:

Create a "Values Hierarchy" list. Rank your top ten values in order of importance. Every goal you make should align with at least your top five values. To help you, I've compiled a list of core values people often identify with.

1. Freedom—choose your own path, live life on your terms.
2. Authenticity—be true to yourself, even when it's uncomfortable.
3. Growth—constant learning to become your best self.
4. Connection—deep, meaningful relationships.
5. Integrity—doing the right thing, even when no one is watching.
6. Health—prioritizing physical, mental, and emotional well-being.
7. Creativity—expressing yourself and thinking outside the box.
8. Contribution—making a difference in the lives of others.
9. Success—achieving meaningful goals and personal milestones.
10. Adventure—seeking new experiences, challenges, and joy.
11. Security—feeling safe, stable, and grounded.
12. Curiosity—staying open to new experiences.
13. Love—giving and receiving a deep emotional connection.
14. Resilience—bouncing back from challenges.
15. Spirituality—connecting to something greater than yourself.

T is for Time-Based: Creating Urgency and Momentum

Without time-based deadlines, goals remain in the realm of "someday," which we all know is not a day that appears on any calendar. Parkinson's Law states that work expands to fill the time allotted for its completion.[16] If you give yourself a week to do a four-hour task, the task will likely take the entire week. You'll fill the extra time with procrastination and overthinking.

By setting clear and appropriate time-based goals, you create a sense of urgency and focus that transforms potential energy into kinetic energy—the energy of motion.

Deadlines create what physicists call "constructive interference." When your daily actions align with your timeline, they amplify each other's effect. This creates momentum, which is the frequency of success in motion.

For example, let's say you can do one push-up, but you want to be able to do 20 push-ups within one month. If you practice doing push-ups every day, you'll reach your goal. But if you wait until the last few days of the month to try to do 20 push-ups, you risk not reaching your goal. Daily practice is the action aligned with your timeline, and it transforms the energy so that you reach your desired goal.

Let's practice:

It's not enough just to set a final deadline. Every goal needs three timeframes:

---

[16] Britannica Editors, ed. "Bureaucracy - Structure, Processes, & Functions | Britannica." C. Northcote Parkinson: British historian and author. Accessed January 7, 2026. https://www.britannica.com/topic/bureaucracy/Bureaucracy-and-the-state.

- Ultimate Deadline: The date you want to achieve the final result.
- Milestone Markers: Interim deadlines that keep you on track.
- Daily Rhythms: What you'll do each day to move toward your goal.

Going back to the push-up example, the Ultimate Deadline is one month, or 30 days. You might choose weekly deadlines for your Milestone Markers. You could check your progress every Saturday and record whether or not you could do more push-ups than the week before. And the Daily Rhythms goal would be the number of push-ups you'll attempt and complete each day.

To make your goals both important (high value) and scarce (limited time), use the Urgency Equation: Urgency = Importance x Scarcity. Remember, if you don't achieve the goal in the timeframe you originally set, you didn't fail. You just set the wrong date or timeframe. Reset the date and keep moving forward!

Let's see how making a time-based goal works with our weight loss example. You'll have three timeframes: the Ultimate Deadline, Milestone Markers, and Daily Rhythms. For weight loss, the ultimate deadline needs to be realistic. You won't be able to lose 20 pounds in a week and be healthy, but you could lose 1 to 2 pounds a week. If you lost one pound per week, it would take 20 weeks to lose 20 pounds. That's your ultimate deadline.

Next, you'll plan a few interim deadlines to keep you on track. At weeks number 5, 10, and 15, you'll check in and make sure you're on track.

Finally, you'll create small, daily goals to keep you moving forward. Daily goals for weight loss could include sticking to an exercise and nutrition plan, along with mental motivation practices like meditation.

Frequency hack:

Imagine you had to achieve your goal in half the time you originally planned. This is called "time compression." What would you do differently? Often, this reveals faster pathways you hadn't previously considered, and it can set your goals on fire!

The SMART Frequency Formula in Action

Now that you understand how SMART goals work, let's transform a common financial goal using the SMART framework:

Non-SMART Goal:

I want to be financially free.

SMART Goal:

I will increase my net worth to $500,000 by December 31, 2027, by saving $2,000 per month, investing in index funds and real estate, and generating $3,000 in monthly passive income through my online course business. I will review and chart my progress every week to see if I'm on track.

Frequency Analysis:

- Specific: Exact dollar amount and methods
- Measurable: $500,000 net worth, $2,000 monthly savings, $3,000 passive income
- Achievable: Based on current income and realistic investment returns
- Relevant: Aligns with desire for financial freedom and security
- Time-based: Clear deadline with implied monthly milestones

The Positive Vibrational Side Effects of Creating SMART Goals

SMART goals shift your frequency and broadcast clarity and momentum out into the world. That frequency not only helps you reach your goals, but also draws your goals toward you.

When you use SMART goals consistently, you'll notice several powerful side effects:

- Amplify clarity: Your decision-making becomes faster and more accurate because you have clear criteria for what moves you toward your goals.
- Increase confidence: Each achieved milestone builds your belief in your ability to achieve the next one, creating an upward spiral of self-assurance.
- Attract opportunities: Clear goals act like a filter, helping you notice opportunities that align with your objectives while ignoring distractions.

- Optimize energy: You waste less energy on activities that don't serve your goals, creating more power for what matters.

These side effects are magnetic. The clearer and more aligned you are with your goals, the more the universe meets you with synchronicity and support.

Four Common SMART Goal Mistakes That Lower Your Success Frequency

SMART goals are powerful, but only when applied with intention. If you set them with the wrong energy, like doubt and skepticism, you'll unintentionally lower your frequency and block the flow.

Here are four common traps to avoid:

1. The Perfection Trap: Waiting for the "perfect" goal before starting. Perfection is a delay tactic dressed up as diligence. A clear, good-enough goal, taken seriously, will beat a perfect goal that never launches.
2. The Isolation Error: Setting goals in isolation from your life context. Your goals should work together like a symphony, not compete like dueling banjos. Consider your relationships, health, energy, and values when goal-setting.
3. The Rigidity Mistake: Refusing to adjust your goals when circumstances change. Rigidity lowers your frequency. Adaptation isn't failure; it's wisdom in motion. SMART goals are meant to be dynamic, not static.
4. The Comparison Contamination: Setting goals based on someone else's path. When you borrow someone

else's dream, you disconnect from your own vibration. Authentic goals generate high-frequency action. Borrowed goals burn out fast.

Remember: SMART goals are a tool, not a rulebook. Use them to tune your energy to a higher frequency. The more your goals reflect your truth, the more potent your vibration becomes.

Your SMART Goal Success Ritual

Use this daily morning and evening ritual to maximize the frequency-aligning power of your SMART goals:

Morning Alignment (Ten Minutes)
- Review your goals
- Visualize achieving them
- Feel the emotions of success
- Identify your top three goal advancing actions for the day

Evening Reflection (Ten Minutes)
- Assess the progress on your goals
- Celebrate the wins, however small
- Adjust tomorrow's actions based on today's learnings
- Express gratitude for movement toward your goals

Your Goals as Frequency Generators

While it's true that SMART goals help you achieve your desired results, they also bring alignment. When you craft goals that are Specific, Measurable, Achievable, Relevant, and Time-based, you are programming your frequency for success.

Your goals become a tuning instrument that helps you dial into the vibration and frequency of your desired life. They create coherent energy patterns to which the universe can respond with precision, transforming scattered hopes and dreams into focused intention, and scattered intention into magnetic attraction.

Remember, the universe doesn't respond to your words. It responds to your thoughts and emotional frequency. Make sure your goals are broadcasting the exact signal you want to receive back. With SMART goals as your frequency tuner, you set the vibrational stage for inevitable success.

The frequency of success is more than outward achievements. It's who you become in the process. SMART goals are the catalyst for both your outer transformation and your inner evolution. Your future self is already vibrating at the frequency of your achieved goals. All you have to do now is tune in.

Assessment: Your Pre-Flight Checklist

These four practices—tenacity, discipline, consistency, and SMART goal-setting—are your foundation. If you skip them or apply them sporadically, you'll struggle. But if you lean into them, you'll gain momentum fast. You'll start building a foundation of high-frequency thinking, which leads to high-frequency beliefs and results.

Just as pilots run through a pre-flight checklist to ensure the plane is ready for takeoff, you can use this simple checklist every morning to raise your frequency and stay aligned with your goals.

1. Am I grounded in my purpose? Why did I start this journey? Am I working daily to achieve this goal?

2. Am I committed to showing up today? Even if I feel tired, discouraged, or distracted, will I show up to the best of my ability?
3. Am I focused on the right things? Am I being disciplined with my time and energy?
4. Am I taking real action? What's one thing I can do today to move me toward my goal?
5. Do I know exactly what I'm working toward? Is my goal SMART, or do I need to revise it?

CHAPTER 6
The Missing Frequency

Chances are, long before you picked up this book, you were practicing personal development. You've likely read self-help books, repeated affirmations, or even kept a gratitude journal. Maybe you made a vision board and looked at it every day. If you caught yourself thinking negative thoughts, you'd quickly turn them around.

You've done the work, but something is still missing. You aren't getting the results you had hoped for.

If it makes you feel better, you're not alone. Most people who feel stuck, frustrated, or like the Universe has ghosted them are doing a lot of things right. But they're doing them without the key element that makes it all work: the frequency behind the action.

You can take all the right steps, practice affirmations daily, visualize your dreams, think positive thoughts, and still not get results if your inner signal isn't aligned. It's like tuning into your favorite radio station. If you're even just a tiny bit off, the signal doesn't come through clearly, and all you get is static.

If this resonates with you, don't worry. The work you've done so far isn't wasted. In this chapter, I'll share why what you've tried before isn't working and how to dial in your efforts so you can receive the breakthroughs you're looking for. Because when you align your focus with a higher frequency, your perspective shifts, and suddenly you not only have clarity, but you also achieve the results you're after. You don't need to start over. You just need to dial it in.

Why It Didn't Work (At Least, Not Long-Term)

Most people approach manifestation this way: They set a goal, think positive thoughts, and visualize it coming to fruition. But if their inner frequency, or self-belief, is still broadcasting fear, frustration, or scarcity, the signal they're sending won't match the results they want.

When you operate from a low-vibrational state, stop practicing consistently, and worry about how you'll reach your goals, you'll sabotage your efforts.

Let's take a closer look at the common reasons why you're not seeing results long-term.

Operating From a Low-Vibrational State

One reason you're not seeing results from the tools you've learned is that you're practicing from a low-vibrational state, such as stress, fear, doubt, and lack. Those are all low-frequency emotions.

Operating at a low-frequency vibration will bring low-frequency results. Raising your vibration to a higher frequency will attract high-frequency results. Remember the Law of Vibration and the principle that like attracts like? If you're not getting the results you want, check your vibrational state and take the necessary steps to raise it. I'll teach you how to do that in chapter 8 with daily mind and body anchoring practices.

Inconsistent Practice

Frequency isn't just energy; it's how often you show up. Raising your frequency means being consistent with your daily practice. Just like going to the gym or learning a new language, you wouldn't expect ripped abs or to speak fluently after only a handful of sessions. It takes targeted and disciplined repetition over time.

It's okay if you miss a session here and there. Life happens, and we all have those days that don't go as planned. But the most successful people don't let a few bad days stop them. They prioritize their practice because they know it's the fastest way to reach their goals.

Focusing on the "How"

When it comes to setting goals and doing visualization exercises to build your self-image and manifest your dreams, people often get stuck in the "how." They worry about *how* it's going to happen instead of believing in the power of the universal mind, or the Law of Universal Oneness. They're obsessed with *how* it's going to happen instead of anchoring in the belief that it *will* happen. They get bogged down, frustrated, and eventually give up because they're worrying about the wrong things.

Please understand that you do not need to know *how* you're going to do it, only that you *are* going to do it. If your "why" is big enough and powerful enough, and you have total belief in your new self-image, the "how" will take care of itself. Your subconscious mind will do the work behind the scenes, the Universal Laws will each play their part, and opportunities will present themselves to you.

Fighting Your Old Self-Image

Your self-image is your view or concept of yourself, and it's a fundamental part of your personality. It determines your general sense of who you are, whether that's intelligent, confident, and successful, or unworthy, anxious, and never good enough. How you see yourself controls virtually all of your successes and failures.

As you work on self-development, you build and develop your self-image into a more positive version. But sometimes that old, outdated version of yourself reaches up and tries to pull you back down like a crab in a bucket. When that happens, it means that there is a misalignment between your internal state and external actions.

Externally, you're doing the work to build your self-image, but internally, it hasn't fully taken root yet. The key is to recognize when this happens so you can address it by spending time restoring your new self-image.

You've Been Doing the Right Work—On the Wrong Wavelength

You've been showing up for yourself, maybe for years now. Listening to podcasts, watching affirmation videos on

YouTube, and even attending workshops. You've invested time, money, and energy into becoming the successful person you want to be, but your front-row seat has brought you no closer to your goals.

First, I commend you for your dedication. It means you're fully committed and not afraid to put in the effort. But here's the hard truth: You can do all the "right" things, but if your frequency isn't aligned, the results will always fall short.

It's not that you've been doing it wrong. It's that you've been doing the right work from the wrong wavelength. You're so close to tuning in that dial, all you need to do is make a few adjustments to raise your frequency.

1. Build Your Self-Belief

The first step is to build your self-belief. That means you have to envision yourself as if you already have what you're striving for. It's not easy to do when your brain is saying, *But you don't really have that yet*, or you're not seeing results fast enough. It's all a matter of raising your frequency. Focus on feeling gratitude for the life you've envisioned by noticing small wins throughout your day and week. Surround yourself with positive influences that uplift you—music, friends, podcasts, or books. Treat yourself the way you'd treat someone you love. Practice self-compassion by acknowledging your efforts and allowing room for mistakes without judgment.

Building self-belief is a process, but as long as you keep moving forward, keep seeing yourself as if you already have what you want, you'll be successful. Lou Holtz, a former college football coach, said, "In this world, you're either growing or dying, so get in motion and grow."[17] If you're moving in the direction of your goals, then you are growing, and that fact alone puts you on the path to success.

2. Believe That Success Isn't a Destination

The next step is to understand that success isn't a destination; it's never the final result. The common definitions of success might lead you to believe that success is a place you aspire to reach or arrive at.

What if I told you that success is not static, but dynamic? What if you didn't have to reach a destination to be successful, but merely moved in the direction of it? The great Earl Nightingale said, "Success is the progressive realization of a worthy goal or ideal."[18] Take a moment to look back on how far you've come. You are already successful in many areas of your life, and it will keep getting better from here.

3. Make Consistent Efforts

At first, reciting your affirmations, making a vision board, and dreaming of a better life are fun and exciting. And after a while, it might feel like things are shifting into a better place.

But then, real life creeps back in. The excitement fades and the old doubts return. You wonder if you missed some critical secret that successful people know but aren't telling you. The truth is, the secret is in the *doing*. Successful people know the importance of consistent effort.

---

[17] "Lou Holtz Quote," *AZ Quotes*, Accessed December 10, 2025, https://www.azquotes.com/quote/349134

[18] "Earl Nightingale Quotes," *BrainyQuote*, Accessed December 10, 2025, https://www.brainyquote.com/quotes/earl_nightingale_383460.

Building the habit of daily, intentional practice takes work. If you miss a few days, make the effort to get back on track because staying in motion and continuing to move forward helps you keep your energy and vibration high. The tools you learned and have been practicing aren't useless. They're just incomplete.

Let's take a look at why what you're doing isn't working.

The Tools Aren't the Problem

The point of this chapter isn't to dismiss the work you've done. The affirmations, meditations, and visualizations haven't failed you. Not completely. The problem isn't the tools; it's the clarity of the lens you're looking through when you use them. If you want the highest probability of success, you have to raise your vibration and frequency.

When you operate from a low-frequency vibration, the affirmations and meditations become empty rituals. Let's say you come to your practice after having a rough day at work or an argument with someone, or maybe you've been anxious and worried about your financial situation. Those emotional states fog up the lens, and they don't have the power to intensify the work you're doing.

But when you come to your practice with positive, happy, and confident emotions, everything sharpens. You've raised your frequency, so those same tools become amplifiers to bring your goals into focus. They help you see possibilities more clearly.

Think of it this way: Your vibration is the lens, and the tools are the camera. You can buy the best, most expensive camera on the market, capable of stunning results. But if the lens is smudged, cracked, or fogged up, the picture will come out distorted. Shift your vibration by cleaning the "lens," and suddenly the camera creates a completely different image, one that is clear and in focus.

That's why two people can do the exact same morning routine and get completely different results. For the person whose "lens" is clean—aligned with joy, gratitude, and belief—the tools become frequency and clarity amplifiers. For the person whose "lens" is clouded with doubt, resentment, or exhaustion, the tools only magnify the distortion and negative energy.

So how do you clean the lens and raise your vibration? It can be as simple as watching a funny video, taking a walk, or dancing to your favorite song. Once you've set your viewfinder on a higher vibration, your world snaps into focus. And *that's* the moment to begin your visualization or meditation practice.

The Real Secret: Build Your Belief

The principles I teach you in this book aren't new. They've been around for thousands of years, but few people really understand them, and even fewer know how to apply them. That's because most education in this field doesn't address how to raise your frequency and vibration.

At the very core of this work is your belief and self-image. The only thing that really matters is what your subconscious mind believes. Once you understand that, your actions will become aligned with your beliefs. You'll start taking intentional action with consistency, and that consistency will build intensity until you're humming along at such a high frequency that the possibilities are endless. You won't believe the speed at which the Universe responds.

What's Next: The FLIGHT Method

Now that you understand what's been missing from your practice—tuning in to higher frequencies—it's time to do something different.

In the next chapter, you'll learn the FLIGHT Method, my step-by-step process for raising your vibration, aligning your actions, and staying in that high-frequency state long enough to create incredible results.

Keep in mind that the FLIGHT Method isn't a quick fix. It's a way of living that makes success feel natural. Once you start using it and embrace the process, the right opportunities will start flowing toward you.

My Vibrational Frequency Self-Assessment Test

Before you turn the page, take a moment to go back to chapter 2 and complete parts 1 and 2 of the My Vibrational Frequency Self-Assessment Test. Compare your results with the results from the first time you took it. Has your score shifted for the better? If not, don't worry—with a little more understanding and intentional practice, it will.

Part 2

THE FREQUENCY OF SUCCESS FRAMEWORK

Your frequency isn't random. When you apply the Frequency of Success Framework, you can learn to master your energy and vibration to manifest anything you want in life.

CHAPTER 7

The FLIGHT Method

Think of this chapter as your boarding pass for a high-frequency life. So far, you've learned how frequency works, how to recognize it, and how to align with the 12 Laws of the Universe. But here's the question: How do you actually lift off?

That's where the FLIGHT Method comes in. Instead of a rigid step-by-step checklist, it's a six-part framework you can return to again and again. It's a set of interconnected practices that work together, designed to raise your energy and vibration, allowing you to create success from the inside out. Each part provides a way to check in with your energy, release what's holding you back, and build the habits that allow you to live in sustained higher frequencies.

Just like a pilot monitors altitude, fuel, and weather conditions, the FLIGHT Method helps you stay aware of your energy, release resistance, make intentional choices, ground yourself in good habits, live in high vibration, and ultimately transform your life through action. Because the truth is, the only way to shift is to lift, and these six principles show you how.

The question is, are you ready to take flight? Let's go.

F: Frequency Awareness

You can't change your altitude if you don't check your instruments. So, the first step to raising your vibration is knowing where you are right now.

Think of energy as a spectrum; it can be low, high, or anywhere in between. At any given moment, your energy falls somewhere on the spectrum. On the low end, you feel negative, drained, or stuck. On the high end, you're in flow, things fall into place, opportunities line up, and you feel like you're on top of the world. For most of us, our energy moves up and down throughout the day, but generally we fall somewhere in the middle.

The goal of frequency awareness is to recognize where you are and intentionally make little shifts that raise your energy and vibration. Simple practices can help. One of the easiest things you can do to improve your vibration immediately is to smile. A genuine, heartfelt smile signals your body to release energy that raises your level. Laughing, listening to good music, feeling gratitude, and immersing yourself in nature all raise your vibration.

On the other hand, you also need to be aware of when your energy and vibration start falling to the negative end of the spectrum. Take note of how you feel in certain environments, such as when listening to the news or when participating in negative conversations. It's easy to get caught up in the trap of scrolling through negative social media feeds and responding to negative comments. It's a nosedive that can be hard to pull out of.

Being aware of your frequency is the foundation of a high-frequency life. As I said, you can't confirm changing your altitude if you don't check your instruments. Once you check in with yourself and know your current vibration, you can decide where to go from there.

Take Action

For the next seven days, check in and monitor or document your frequency at least twice a day—once in the morning and once in the evening. Simply ask yourself, "Where am I on the energy spectrum right now? Low, midrange, or high?" Then choose one small action to raise your vibration in that moment:

- Smile.
- Go for a walk.
- Listen to uplifting music.
- Step outside and notice nature.
- List three things you're grateful for.
- Dance around for two minutes.
- Watch a funny video.
- Give or receive a heartfelt hug.
- Give a compliment to a stranger.

As you experience these options, make a note in your journal detailing how you became aware of your frequency and how you shifted your state of vibration.

L: Let Go of Resistance

Planes can't take off if they're overloaded. The same is true for your energy. Resistance, in the form of old beliefs, toxic habits, and unresolved emotions, acts like extra baggage that weighs you down.

One of the most common limiting beliefs is "I can't." That phrase shuts down the possibility before it even begins. Try reframing it to "How can I?" It's a small change in language that opens your mind to solutions and invites energy to flow again.

Letting go often requires conscious intention. Implementing positive practices into your daily routine can help. For instance, journaling helps you uncover patterns and explore stories you've carried for years. Breathwork clears emotional tension stored in the body. Forgiveness releases resentments that quietly drain you.

Every time you release resistance, you free up energy for growth. Think of it as dropping excess cargo so your plane can finally lift off.

Take Action

Identify one belief, habit, or story that has been weighing you down. Write it in your journal and challenge it with this question: *What if the opposite were true?*

For the next 30 days, practice replacing the old belief with a new statement of possibility. For example, replace "I can't make $10,000 a month," with "How can I make $10,000 a month?" Notice how your energy shifts as you release that resistance and get curious about the new possibilities that will be showing up, seemingly out of thin air.

I: *Intentional Input*

Energy is always moving. It's all around you, and it's always changing. The question is: What kind of energy are you letting in?

If you don't already understand, what you consume—food, media, conversations, environments—directly affects your frequency. If your daily input includes a huge dose of negativity, you shouldn't be surprised when your vibration stays low. You can protect your energetic field by setting boundaries and erecting energetic guardrails that support you.

The most important energetic guardrail is to be intentional. Choose books, podcasts, and mentors that uplift you. Spend time with people who challenge and encourage you. Eat foods that make you feel energized rather than sluggish. Pay attention to the thoughts you repeat to yourself and the type of self-talk you engage in. All of these are inputs that can raise or lower your vibration.

Intentional input is like putting coordinates into your navigation system. It keeps you on course toward a higher frequency.

Take Action

At the end of this week, do a quick "energy audit." In your journal or on a piece of paper, make two columns and label them Energy Depleters and Energy Replenishers. In the Energy

Depleters column, list the foods, shows, conversations, people, or anything that drains your energy. In the second column, list the inputs that lift you up and provide positive moments in your day.

Then, commit to swapping out at least one depleting input for one replenishing input every day for the next 30 days. Even small substitutions like choosing an apple instead of binging on chocolate bars or a ten-minute walk instead of scrolling through news stories can make a noticeable difference in your frequency. Feel free to use the list of options from the Take Action step under Frequency Awareness to fill up your Energy Replenishers.

As you're performing your energy audit, you might notice that some items, like eating chocolate or watching a show, could be an Energy Depleter or an Energy Replenisher. It all depends on how they make you feel in that moment. Sometimes, indulging in a piece of chocolate or watching a show with a loved one can lift you up. But other times, it could drain your energy, depending on why you're participating in the action at that moment. The important thing is to take notice of your frequency and always work to intentionally improve it.

G: *Grounded Growth*

Growth is what stabilizes your flight; it provides the foundation for sustained success. How do you continue to grow? You commit to being a student. Grounded growth occurs when you purposefully work on self-improvement and personal development.

- Read, listen, and learn from people who have gone before you.
- Build a personal "library" of books, tools, and insights that help you expand your knowledge.
- Practice daily actions that raise your frequency.

Growth comes from consistent habits over time. Can you raise your vibration in 30 or 60 days? Certainly, but real growth, the kind that creates massive shifts, only comes from consistent, intentional attention and practice. It's not a frantic frenzy of obtaining all the answers as fast as you can. Instead, it's a steady, grounded development that changes your self-image over time.

Daily nonnegotiable actions that stabilize high-frequency living make the difference. These don't have to be hard. It's the simple practices like gratitude, movement, stillness, learning, belief, and action that keep your frequency stable and growing. Even a few minutes a day create a strong foundation that can withstand the negative forces you'll encounter. Grounded habits are what keep your energy strong when life gets turbulent.

Take Action

Create a simple list of resources—your personal "flight library"—to keep track of the tools, books, and insights that speak to you. Then pick one or two books, podcasts, or courses that support your growth and commit to engaging with them over the next 30 days. Even a few minutes each day can help you transform.

To grow faster, choose one daily nonnegotiable habit (meditation, movement, stillness, gratitude journaling, etc.)

and practice it consistently. Growth happens when you stack small, consistent, positive habits that stabilize your energy and vibration.

H: *High-Vibe Output*

Have you ever noticed how some people have a distinct energy that seems to precede them everywhere they go? When they enter a room, you can feel the energy shift, whether it's a positive, energetic buzz or a depressive feeling. That's how powerful your frequency can be. High-vibe output is about aligning your inner world so that the vibration and energy you send out elevates the spaces you're in, and hopefully in a good way. Nobody wants to be the person who sucks the life out of a room—trust me on this one.

Achieving inner balance for a higher vibrational output is accomplished through meditation and visualization. Spending 10 to 15 minutes seeing yourself at your best raises your frequency. In this practice, employ all of your senses. Visualize the images, feel the emotions, listen to the sounds, and remember the scents and fragrances. In your mind, fully immerse yourself in the visualization to reconnect to that frequency.

It's critical that you visualize yourself already in possession of the success that you seek. This is how the subconscious mind will begin to create your new reality. The more you make this visualization real in your mind, the faster you will see the new reality manifest in your life.

Having a high-vibe output is like a thermostat. Instead of reacting to the temperature around you, be the one to set it. If others are complaining or draining the energy in the room, you can choose to respond differently. You can move the dial and change the vibration not only for yourself, but also for everyone around you. When your energy is high and aligned, you naturally create harmony wherever you go.

Take Action

Set aside ten minutes each day this week for a visualization practice. First, choose one goal or dream that you want to bring into reality. It could be something like landing your dream job, buying a house, finding that perfect someone, or traveling to a tropical destination.

Whatever it is, make sure to engage all five senses as you visualize yourself reaching your goal or receiving your dream. What do you see, hear, feel, smell, and taste in that high-frequency version of you? Imagine all the details, as if you were already there, as if you'd already achieved it. Visualizing right before sleep is one of the best ways to let your subconscious mind take charge and start bringing that dream closer and closer to reality.

T: *Transformation Through Takeoff & Traction*

Transformation happens when all of these steps come together. You can't pick and choose to only practice the easiest ones. Awareness, release, intention, growth, and high frequency all lead to takeoff. This is where momentum builds and results compound exponentially.

I know I've said this before, and you've heard it throughout the book, but the key is consistency. A single burst of effort won't sustain you. Just like an airplane requires steady thrust to climb, transformation requires repeated, aligned action. The amount of effort it takes to achieve success will *not* be enough to keep you there. You have to keep working. When you commit, you gain traction, and each success lifts your frequency even higher. But if you stop, you'll end up losing traction, stalling, and even sliding backward.

Frequency awareness comes into play as you pay attention to your feedback loops. Who do you spend time with? Do they raise your vibration or drain your energy? What results are you seeing? If progress stalls, check your environment, habits, or mindset. Just as a pilot makes constant adjustments mid-flight, you can correct course whenever you need to.

Use the My Vibrational Frequency Self-Assessment Test from chapter 2 anytime you feel like you've lost momentum and need to get back on course. You can also track your daily mood, energy, and frequency levels in a diary or journal. Over time, you'll see patterns that help you adjust faster.

I've said it before, and I'll keep saying it...transformation is not a one-time event but a process of *consistent* elevation. Remember, the runway is where confidence builds. Takeoff is when you commit.

Take Action

At the end of each day for the next 30 days, do a quick FLIGHT Check to ensure that you've taken action on raising your energy and vibration.

Ask yourself:

- Did I notice my frequency today?
- Did I let go of at least one resistance?
- Did I choose intentional inputs?
- Did I grow in some way?
- Did I share high-vibe output?

Keep it simple. Five check marks in a notebook are enough. Over time, these daily micro-checks will build the momentum that fuels lasting transformation, and they give you an easy visual representation of your progress. Success happens in small increments.

Ready to Fly

Raising your vibration is about simple daily actions, and the FLIGHT Method gives you a grounded, repeatable way to do that:

- Frequency Awareness
- Let Go of Resistance
- Intentional Input
- Grounded Growth
- High-Vibe Output
- Transformation

Together, these six elements form a system you can return to daily. When you apply the FLIGHT Method, you create momentum that lifts you beyond doubt, burnout, and limitations. You become the kind of person whose energy leads the way.

Remember the Wright brothers? They didn't invent flight. But they believed that powered flight was possible. They kept showing up, testing, adjusting, and refining until they finally achieved liftoff. The same is true for you. Transformation is built through consistent action, intentional choices, and a willingness to keep going every time you falter.

The FLIGHT Method helps you lift off and keeps you flying to greater heights.

So, keep checking your "thermostat," monitoring your energy, and releasing what no longer serves you. Choose inputs and habits that sustain your frequency, and keep showing up with high-vibe outputs. Build your FLIGHT ritual, and when the runway calls—commit.

Because the only way to shift is to lift. With the FLIGHT Method, you now have the tools to do it.

Next Stop On the FLIGHT Plan

After putting into practice the six principles of the FLIGHT Method, you have likely experienced how simple daily shifts create lift. But the real test is keeping the airplane in the air.

In the next chapter, we'll talk about the critical components that make high-frequency living sustainable: consistency and disciplined practice. You'll discover the daily practices and techniques that anchor your energy and create the momentum that transforms temporary lift-offs into a transcontinental flight.

CHAPTER 8

Practices That Sustain High-Frequency Living

High-frequency living isn't a state that you just visit every now and then; it's a state you live in. Attending a weekend workshop or motivational seminar can give you a temporary boost, but what happens when the weekend is over? Without the high energy of the event motivating you, it's easy to slip back into old patterns.

This is why consistency and disciplined practice are critical. Without them, the FLIGHT Method is like an aircraft without fuel—impressive in design, but unable to lift off the runway. With consistency and disciplined practice as your fuel, you develop the ability to live in alignment with your highest frequency as your default setting.

In this chapter, we'll explore the practices that keep you steady in turbulent times. You'll see how the mind and body work together to regulate frequency, how consistency creates momentum, and how daily habits like meditation, nutrition, and sleep shape the energy you bring to every area of your life. We'll also look at how frequency influences business, leadership, and financial success.

If you've ever wondered why some people seem to effortlessly attract opportunities, the answer is this: They've mastered what's in this chapter. They don't just visit high frequency—they live there. And by the end of the chapter, you'll know how to do the same.

Frequency Fundamentals

Most days, high-frequency living is fun and exciting! You spend a lot of time in the flow, and opportunities often come knocking. It's easy to stay consistent with your practices when life is going smoothly. But what about when turbulence hits? What happens when you wake up in a low-frequency mood that you can't quite shake, your relationships feel strained, and for some reason, those opportunities just aren't showing up like they used to?

Difficult days are the real test of high-frequency life. How do you respond when life gets hard? The answer is two-fold: You must take consistent, disciplined action, and then you must course correct.

Taking Consistent Disciplined Action

The first step in getting back into the flow is to identify your current baseline frequency. Ask yourself: Where do I naturally operate most days—low, neutral, or high? If you're not sure, go back to chapter 2 and retake the My Vibrational Frequency Self-Assessment Test. Your results will give you a clear picture of where you're starting from. Once you know your baseline, the goal is to raise it gradually so that your new "normal" becomes a higher standard of energy and vibration. This doesn't happen in one big leap. It happens through small daily practices, consistently repeated.

Course Correcting

Once you've determined your vibrational frequency, whether it's negative, neutral, or positive, it's time to course correct. When turbulence hits and knocks you off course, you need the ability to course correct quickly.

Think of a pilot navigating around a storm. If the plane is on autopilot, it'll fly straight into turbulence. But if the pilot proactively adjusts the course, he can steer toward clearer skies. High-frequency practices are those course corrections and keep you flying steady, even when life blows unexpected storms your way.

Practices to Sustain High-Frequency Living

You're probably wondering what daily practices you need to implement to get back on course. We'll start with mind and body practices that raise your vibration. Then, we'll dive into achieving high-frequency success in business and financial abundance.

I'm going to give you a great deal of information in the following pages, so don't be afraid to take it slow. The best way to grasp the information is to read it and then implement the practices into your daily routine. But don't try to do everything at once. Pick one practice to work on, stay consistent with it, and then add the next practice.

Are you ready to earn your wings? Let's go!

Raising Your Frequency Through Mind Practices

Your thoughts are the control tower of your energy and vibration, and every pattern of thinking either raises or lowers your vibration. Let's explore how your mind, both consciously and subconsciously, affects your frequency.

Elevate or Lower Your Vibration with Thought Patterns

Low-frequency thought patterns can be subtle but powerful. Even small habits can shift our vibration and completely change our outlook. For instance, the first thing most people do in the morning is check their phone. They scroll through social media, catch up on the news, and start worrying about finances.

The wasted time spent scrolling means they are late getting out the door. So they grab a sugary, caffeinated drink on the way to work instead of nourishing their body with a healthy breakfast. As they frantically weave through traffic, they can't remember if they fed the dog and closed the garage door on their mad dash out of the house.

They begin their day participating in the endless stream of negativity, which puts them in a low vibrational state. As you can see, this practice can quickly spiral out of control, putting them in a deep negative pit that is tough to climb out of.

So, what can you do? I propose a simple solution. Begin a "media fast." For 30 days, cut out all media influences. Hide or turn off all social media on your phone, stop watching the news, and remove any other negative media from your daily routine.

At first, this will feel almost impossible. You'll catch yourself reaching for your phone twenty times a day out of pure habit. You might even feel anxious, like you're missing out or falling behind because you don't know what's happening in the world. But guess what? The world will continue to turn on its axis whether you're keeping tabs on it or not. And anything that is meant to find you, will.

After a few days, you'll notice your mind feels lighter. By the end of the first week, you'll start to reclaim the focus and energy you didn't realize you were missing. And by day 30, you'll wonder why you ever let so many outside influences dictate your mood, your focus, and most of all, your frequency.

A media fast is a great start. But what if you took it a step further? Now that you've removed the negativity, what if you replaced it with positivity? I'm talking about listening to inspirational and motivational talks, journaling, participating in small acts of kindness, and beginning your day with gratitude and meditation. These small choices program your mind to see the good around you and expect possibilities rather than problems and frantic chaos.

Reprogram Your Subconscious Mind

Most of the results in your life start with what's hidden in your subconscious mind. In chapter 4, we talked about how limiting beliefs are the first obstacle to raising your frequency. If your subconscious is full of limiting beliefs, no amount of reciting hollow affirmations will change it. To see consistent and lasting change in your life, you need to reprogram your subconscious mind, essentially rebuilding your self-image. Reprogramming begins with cognitive restructuring—replacing negative inputs with positive ones. It involves creating new neural pathways.

New neural pathways are created by spending more time in high-frequency thinking and less time in low-frequency thinking. Admittedly, restructuring your subconscious is easier said than done. It takes constant, conscious daily effort. But when you consciously change the input by replacing old patterns with empowering ones, you redirect your subconscious toward new destinations.

This is what it means to course correct. Just like the pilot who course corrected to avoid the storm, you can change your flight pattern. Maybe you catch yourself slipping into self-doubt before a big meeting and pause to remind yourself of past wins instead. Or you notice negative self-talk creeping in, and you consciously replace it with something positive about yourself. Or perhaps you notice that the conversation is turning toward gossip, so you step away and turn on a motivational podcast instead of engaging.

You're the pilot of your subconscious mind. Being proactive about adding positive, high-frequency inputs to your mind creates new neural pathways over time, so you can go from rain and thunderstorms to clear, blue skies.

Practice Meditation and Mindfulness

Now that you understand how critical it is to reprogram your subconscious and manage your thought patterns, let's explore some everyday practices you can stash in your flight plan to stay consistent.

Two of the most powerful practices are meditation and mindfulness. Both are talked about often in personal development circles, but few people truly understand the difference or how to use them together to sustain high-frequency living.

Meditation is the practice of training the mind to achieve a state of calmness, focus, and awareness. It's time set apart from your day for intentional stillness. Meditation can include visualization, deep breathing, or prayer, and it can be practiced for as little as five minutes. A simple meditation technique is to sit in a comfortable position, close your eyes if you'd like, and bring your attention to your breath as you steadily inhale and exhale. When thoughts come up, simply notice them and gently return your focus to your breath and visualization. The key to meditation is to fully involve all of your senses. Visualize the results you desire, feel the emotions as if they are already real, and let your body experience the outcome as if it has already happened.

Mindfulness, on the other hand, is the moment-to-moment awareness you carry throughout your day. It's often called "being present." It's pausing to ask: *Where is my frequency right now? Am I slipping into low energy and vibration, or am I maintaining alignment with higher frequencies?* Mindfulness also means evaluating your choices: *Will going out to the club after work get me closer to or further away from my goals?*

Sometimes, an outside source can alter your vibration. Maybe you receive bad news, or someone cuts you off in traffic. When that happens, mindfulness helps you choose how to respond rather than react.

Meditation and mindfulness are closely related. When used together, they become a powerful part of your daily practice. Start by setting aside five to ten minutes each morning to quiet your mind and visualize your desired outcomes. Then, carry that high-frequency energy into your day through mindfulness. Pause regularly to check your vibration, notice when outside distractions pull you off course, and choose to recenter and realign with a higher frequency. To round out your day, perform a second meditation session at night before bed.

Use Affirmations and Visualizations (That Actually Work)

We've explored meditation and mindfulness as ways to rewire your subconscious and raise your frequency. Another way to make this change is through repetition paired with emotional impact and visualization. As you now know, in order to make any change in your physical reality, whether it's a change in relationship, career, income, or social status, there must first be a change in the subconscious mind.

Repeating affirmations only works when combined with emotion and sensory involvement. That's why many people dismiss the value of affirmations. They've only experienced them on a rote level, repeating empty words with no feeling. The subconscious isn't moved by words alone. It's moved by repetition plus emotion through visualization. If done correctly, visualization might be the most powerful and effective tool in creating success because to achieve any success in life, you must first be able to see it clearly in your mind.

If you say, "I am rich," but don't feel rich, your subconscious rejects it. But when you create a vivid mental picture of your rich life, add strong emotion through feeling that you are already rich, and repeat it daily, your subconscious begins to accept the new identity. With this practice, you are rewiring your brain, creating new neural pathways, and building a new self-image.

When I first got involved in the network marketing industry, I could never have imagined that in less than one year, I would be the top income earner, let alone earn over $100,000 profit in one month. But then, I began practicing affirmations and visualizations. I let my imagination take flight and slowly reprogrammed my subconscious to a new level of self-belief.

I spent time every day affirming my intentions to the universe. I would read my affirmations in the morning when I woke up, two or three times during the day, and then again before I went to sleep. Seven months after starting, I earned over $103,000 profit in a single month, in addition to landing the company's top income earner award. Some of my affirmations included:

- I am a multiple six-figure income earner, and I help people all over the world improve the quality of their lives. (Notice the part about "helping other people.")
- I am the top income earner in my company.
- I drive a beautiful E55 AMG Mercedes, and I live in a beautiful home with a beautiful view.

Remember, it wasn't just the affirmations that allowed me to manifest these goals into physical reality. I associated strong positive feelings with each one. I visualized myself in each new reality. In my mind, I saw my bank account grow, I felt the smooth, leather seats of the Mercedes, and I visualized myself sitting on the deck of my beautiful home, taking in the expansive view while enjoying the sounds of nature.

Notice how each affirmation is written in the present tense—as if I already am, as if I already have. And while I recited my affirmations, I engaged my senses and acted as if I were there in the moment, like I had already accomplished these wishes. Performing affirmations in this manner tells your subconscious that this is your new reality. And your subconscious has no choice but to believe what you tell it.

Raising Your Frequency Through Body Practices

Now that we've covered how to raise your frequency through mind practices, it's time to tackle the next part of the equation. The mind may be the control tower, but the body is the airplane. Both are necessary for a safe takeoff, flight, and landing.

The mind and body are inseparable when it comes to energy and vibration. If your body is tired, sluggish, and foggy, your ability to maintain high-frequency thoughts and actions is limited. That's because the body sends constant signals to the brain. When your body feels strong and energized, it's easier to think clearly and stay positive. The reverse is also true. When your mind is filled with stress, doubt, and worry, your body feels it. You might get a stomach ache, feel drained, or tense up. The two are always talking to each other, so when you take care of your body, you automatically help your mind operate at a higher frequency and vice versa.

Here are four body practices you can use to consistently raise your frequency.

Leverage the Mind-Body Connection

Exercise is essential for a healthy mind-body connection because your physical and mental states are interconnected. Most people exercise to improve their physical body, but the truth is that physical activities boost vibrational energy, giving your brain a lift too. Movement creates energy, so every time you move your body, you amplify your frequency.

The word "exercise" might be conjuring up visions of slogging out miles on a treadmill or fighting the gym bros for your turn at the squat rack. If that's your vibe, go for it. But what I mean by "exercise" is just getting your body moving in whatever way feels best to you.

Go for a walk, a bike ride, or a swim. Join a game of pickup basketball or dance in your living room. It doesn't matter what activity you do; all that matters is that you get up and move throughout the day. That one action will boost your energy and your brain.

Understand Nutrition and How It Produces Energy

Food is fuel, and your vibration is determined by the fuel you choose. Sugar spikes and processed foods lead to energy crashes, while fresh fruits and vegetables, lean proteins, and whole grains sustain your energy and keep your vibration humming.

So, what does this look like in real life? The key is not to overhaul your diet overnight. Big changes made too quickly often lead to overwhelm and burnout. Instead, start small and build momentum over time. This is where starting small is greatly beneficial.

For instance, you could add one extra piece of fruit to your meal each day this week. Then, swap a soda for water once or twice a week. Once you've created those new habits, try introducing a new vegetable. Little by little, these small changes add up. Drink plenty of water and consider having a blood panel done to identify any potential deficiencies. Supplementation is a great way to counter any known deficits. As your nutritional habits change, you'll experience sustained energy levels, and your recovery time will improve because your body is getting the nutrients it needs.

Master Sleep and Recovery

Just as the physical body repairs and rebuilds while you sleep, the subconscious mind works similarly. Whatever your mind consumes during the day, and especially right before bed, gets processed and reinforced overnight. Poor self-image is one of the greatest enemies of success. That's why meditating and practicing your affirmations and visualizations before you sleep is so powerful. By preparing your mind, you'll not only increase your vibration, but you'll also reprogram your self-image while you sleep. Sleep gives your subconscious time to build and strengthen the new self-image you're building.

Uplevel Your Environment

Finally, consider your environment and how it's impacting your frequency. Living in stressful surroundings, like noisy traffic, negative workplaces, or unsafe neighborhoods, can chip away at your baseline frequency. While you can't always control external conditions, you can design a peaceful microenvironment. A microenvironment is the small space or atmosphere you intentionally create to support your energy. It's your own personal zone of calm and high frequency. It might be a peaceful nook in your home, listening to uplifting music in your car, or wearing noise-canceling headphones at work. These small practices protect your energy and maintain your vibration.

High-Frequency Success in Business and Career

When it comes to living a high-frequency lifestyle, your professional life is no different from your personal life. Your desire to increase your frequency shouldn't get checked at the office door.

When you raise your personal vibration, that higher energy carries over into your professional life. You don't need separate strategies for each area; your business and career will naturally benefit from raising your frequency at home. It's like the idea that a rising tide lifts all ships. When you raise your vibration in one area, you raise it across all areas of your life. It's intertwined.

If you truly love what you do for work, you'll automatically live at a higher frequency at work and at home. However, if you don't love your job, the negativity that comes from performing a job you don't enjoy can spill over into your personal life. That's why it's important to pay attention to your energy.

Raising Your Leadership Energy

If your goal is to become a better leader, start by visualizing yourself as one. If you lack confidence in your leadership abilities, you can "borrow" confidence from other areas of your life where you already excel. Then, take that borrowed confidence and act as if you are the self-assured leader you want to be. Write down the traits of a good leader, and embody them in your daily interactions. Over time, your self-image will naturally shift as your subconscious mind believes that you really are a confident leader.

Raising the Frequency of Teams

Teams reflect the energy of their leader. If you emit low energy, your team will mirror that, and it can negatively affect performance. But when you raise your vibration and consistently operate at a high frequency, your energy naturally elevates theirs, leading to better results.

In every team, there's always that one person who breeds negativity and drains the momentum of the team. These "energy vampires" deplete the team's overall energy and bring down the frequency, which can tank productivity and lead to low morale. If you have an energy vampire on your team, you'll want to address it. You don't need to remove every challenging person, but you do need to set boundaries and lead by example.

You can counteract the energy vampire effect by leading with positivity. The higher your energy, the more it ripples outward, inspiring your team to raise their frequency.

High-Frequency Success in Financial Abundance

Raising your frequency at work and in your career can certainly open the door to more abundance. When it comes to receiving and maintaining financial abundance, the main reason more people aren't wealthy is that their frequency is not aligned with abundance and wealth. If your energy is tuned to scarcity, you'll continue attracting debt, lack, and need. But when you align with the vibration of abundance, opportunities, resources, and wealth begin to flow naturally into your life. This is the classic Law of Attraction in action.

Understanding The Vibration of Money

Money is energy. Money is neither good nor bad. It's simply a tool that allows you to extend the good you do for other people far beyond your physical reach. It carries a vibration just like everything else. And the vibration you send out can either attract or repel it. If you live in scarcity, with limiting beliefs about money, you'll repel it. But if you raise your vibration and believe that money is abundant and available, your energy will be aligned, and you'll attract more.

So, how do you raise your vibration and belief about money? It's pretty simple in practice. When you elevate your vibration through gratitude, generosity, or consistent high-frequency habits, your financial vibration rises with it.

If you want a simple place to start, practice gratitude for the money you already have, no matter the amount. Celebrate every dollar that flows in and appreciate the purpose of every dollar spent and what it provides for you. Gratitude dispels scarcity and attracts abundance.

Breaking Low-Frequency Money Beliefs

Most people inherit limiting beliefs about money during childhood. If you think about it, you can probably remember your parents or grandparents saying something like, "Money doesn't grow on trees," or "We can't afford a fancy house," or even, "Rich people are greedy." These early paradigms shape how we perceive money as adults and often trap us in scarcity thinking.

But you don't have to accept low-frequency money beliefs. The key is to notice when they sneak into your thoughts and replace them with new ones. In a sense, the limiting beliefs and scarcity stories you've been telling yourself are affirmations—negative affirmations. Instead, start repeating positive affirmations about money. Don't forget to infuse your practice with positive emotions.

Try these:

- Money is energy.
- Money allows me to expand the good I do.
- Money flows to me easily.
- I make wise and prosperous financial decisions.
- My wealth grows every day with gratitude.
- I attract opportunities that create financial success.
- I am financially secure and free.

- Abundance, prosperity, and wealth flow into my life every day.

Over time, you'll reprogram your brain. Your subconscious mind will let go of scarcity thinking and embrace an abundance mindset. And that's when the Law of Attraction is activated.

Finding Your Money Ceiling and Seeing Money in Motion

Another example of scarcity thinking is called a "money ceiling." It's an idea many people unconsciously hold that they can't surpass a certain level of income because deep down, they don't believe they deserve more.

Raising your money ceiling starts with creating a new self-image, one that feels worthy and deserving of more. And the way to build your new self-image is to put into consistent practice the teachings from this book.

Money also loves motion. Remember, money is energy. It moves. It vibrates. It's always flowing and exchanging hands. If you want more money, be generous with what you have. Donate to your favorite charities, pay it forward in the grocery line, invest in people and opportunities, do something for someone with nothing expected in return.

Circulating money in meaningful ways attracts more of it back to you. What you put out in the universe returns to you. This is especially true of money. You cannot help others if you are stuck in lack. By raising your vibration about money and putting it in motion, you expand your capacity to help others.

Frequency Check-Ins

High-frequency living isn't a one-time decision. It's a daily practice. Just like a pilot checks the instruments throughout the flight, you need regular frequency check-ins.

Each day, ask yourself:

- How did I start my day?
- Did I begin with gratitude and thanksgiving, or by consuming negative inputs like the news or social media?
- Was I able to reverse low-vibration moments and raise my frequency?

Revisit the My Vibrational Frequency Self-Assessment Test from chapter 2 and compare your results. Are you shifting into higher frequencies?

Progress comes from awareness and persistence. Every time you check in and course correct, you strengthen your ability to live at higher frequencies as your natural state.

Practice Creates Progress

Consistency is not glamorous. No one's going to cheer for you every time you complete your morning meditation or choose to breathe deeply instead of reacting in anger. But these small, disciplined practices are the foundation of transformation.

High-frequency living is not about perfection. It's about progress. Every time you check in and recommit to your practices, you strengthen your energy and vibration. Over time, those small shifts compound into extraordinary results.

Remember, your subconscious mind is always listening. Every affirmation done with emotion, every visualization, and every positive choice changes the programming of your brain. Instead of running on autopilot, you're actively living in a new state of alignment where abundance is normal.

These practices are the critical component of the FLIGHT Method. When you embrace consistency and take disciplined action, you rewrite your future. And once you're living in high-frequency, there is no limit to how far you can fly. Ready for take off?

Part 3

HOW TO RAISE YOUR FREQUENCY

One aligned action a day can change the entire trajectory of your frequency…and your life.

CHAPTER 9
Clear the Interference

Life is full of noise. Endless notifications ping your devices throughout the day, and sometimes well into the night, social media platforms distract you while stealing precious minutes, and the ever-present demands of work and family buzz beneath it all.

Your daily schedule is filled to the brim with work, personal, and family responsibilities. Work emails and texts often call for your attention even after you've clocked out. Daily chores, errands, kids, pets, grocery shopping…it all takes a toll.

Then there are the noises that are not so obvious—the conversation that leaves you doubting yourself, the internal dialogue whispering "you're not good enough," or the stress that follows you out of a tense meeting.

All of this noise creates interference. And interference is the number one cause of frequency interruptions.

You've already learned that raising your frequency and vibration doesn't happen by accident. It happens through deliberate and consistent practice. But to live a high-frequency life, you first have to clear or manage the interference. Otherwise, even the best intentions will get scrambled before you ever reach the runway.

This chapter explores the concept of resistance and how it shows up in the form of external and internal interference. You'll learn how to overcome it through applying the FLIGHT Method and practicing the discipline of situational awareness. Pilots, athletes, and military leaders all depend on situational awareness to perform under pressure. The same principle applies to you and your frequency, regardless of your situation. Without it, you're flying blind. With it, you can navigate turbulence and stay on course no matter what life throws your way.

Why Resistance Shows Up

Resistance is part of human nature. If you've ever said, "I'll start Monday," you've met resistance. If you sat down to work on your goals, but then got "distracted" by your to-do list, you've met resistance. Resistance is low-frequency energy, and it stems from a scarcity mindset.

Resistance can look like:

- Fear: What if I fail?
- Procrastination: I'll do it later.
- Lack of resources: I don't have the time or money right now.

Often, resistance goes beyond your inner thoughts and arises from your external world. Have you ever noticed how the people around you can influence your mood? Resistance emanates from those you surround yourself with and the energy they bring.

If you're surrounded by people who constantly complain, exhibit attitudes of lack and scarcity, or are generally negative, your frequency can suffer, and the negative energy they're putting out will drain you. The energy vampires strike again!

That's why protecting your frequency from interference is just as important as protecting your health. Just like you wouldn't drink polluted water, you can't afford to let polluted energy fill your world.

How to Recognize External Interference

We spend a large part of our time with family members, close friends, and coworkers, so it's important to be aware of the energy they bring. The people closest to you often mean well, but they can unintentionally pull you down.

- A parent who constantly questions your career decision.
- A spouse who simply asks, "Is that realistic?"
- A sibling who rolls their eyes and scoffs when you talk about your dreams.
- Friends who pressure you to join in on gossip or unhealthy habits.
- Coworkers who thrive on office drama and negativity.

External resistance often shows up in small but powerful ways. Imagine you're having a nice dinner with your family—something you don't get to do often. It feels good to reconnect and catch up, but halfway through the meal, you notice doubt creeping in. Suddenly, you're questioning your goals and second-guessing your dreams. That's when you realize some of your family members are energy vampires.

Or maybe you're out with a friend and share an exciting new business idea. Instead of being supportive and cheering you on, they immediately list all the reasons why your idea will never work. The negativity may not be intentional on their part, and it doesn't have to be. They might simply be trying to protect you from a losing proposition, but you internalize it to mean something completely different.

Energy vampires are subtle and sneaky. They look for even the smallest crack in your armor and once they find it, they drain your energy fast. When you find energy being drained by external forces, it's nice to have a few strategies at hand.

Try using these strategies to clear external interference:

- Set clear boundaries.
- Decide in advance what type of conversations you won't engage in. If someone is spiraling into negativity, change the subject or exit gracefully.
- Be strategic with your time.
- Limit the amount of energy you give to draining relationships. You don't have to cut everyone out, but you do need to choose wisely.
- Create exit strategies.
- Plan phrases or actions that let you step away without drawing attention to yourself. "Well, I've got to get back to work" is a simple one.
- Prune your circle if needed.

You'll know when to prune your circle when someone consistently drains your energy (an energy vampire), dismisses your goals, or leaves you feeling depleted and unsteady. Sometimes protecting your energy requires distance. If it's a family member or colleague you can't avoid, set clear boundaries and limit their emotional access to you. Stepping away doesn't mean you don't care; it means you're committed to living a high-frequency life.

How to Recognize Internal Interference

Sometimes, the strongest interference doesn't come from outside; it comes from within. Internal interference is sneaky. It often comes disguised as "logic" or "reality."

Internal interference originates from the voice in your head and might sound something like this:

- "You've tried that before and failed."
- "Other people are good at that, but not you."
- "You'd better play it safe. You don't want to embarrass yourself."

None of those statements will help raise your frequency. They're just the limiting beliefs and old conditioning you've been programmed to run for years, often without realizing it. Left unchecked, internal interference will keep you from ever taking off.

How do you catch internal interference before it drags you down? Once again, you need to put some strategies in place:

Engage in daily personal development inputs. Read, listen to, and watch content that raises your frequency. Even just one podcast, one chapter of a book, or one encouraging conversation can shift your internal narrative and set the tone for the rest of the day.

Perform frequency checks. Pause throughout the day to check in with yourself. Do you feel happy, creative, and energetic? Or are you stuck in overwhelm, letting your mind spin out of control with scarcity thinking? Wherever you are on the frequency spectrum, take a moment to think or act your way to a higher frequency.

Write down your thoughts. Writing out your thoughts reveals patterns you might not otherwise catch. Writing also helps you process your thoughts, allowing you to see possibilities or opportunities.

How to Use The FLIGHT Method to Clear Interference

Whether you're dealing with resistance in the form of internal or external interference, the FLIGHT Method can help. Any time you feel interference blocking your signal, stop and run through the framework.

1. Frequency Awareness

Pause and ask:

- What am I thinking right now?
- Are my thoughts raising my frequency or draining my energy?

- Is my environment raising or lowering my frequency and vibration?

2. Let Go of Resistance

When you realize your frequency is blocked or fading, identify which thoughts or actions are creating the sticking point and then deliberately change or release them.

3. Intentional Input

Do a quick "energy audit" to identify your Energy Depleters and Energy Replenishers. What can you do right now to raise your vibration and replenish your energy? Do you need to listen to something uplifting, have a good laugh, or move your body?

4. Grounded Growth

When you find yourself in a situation where you need to raise your frequency quickly, it's handy to have a positive affirmation or mantra that you can repeat, something that helps you remember your goals. Many people have affirmations as a screensaver on their devices. If possible, go for a quick walk while repeating affirmations.

5. High-Vibe Output

Remember that you want to be the thermostat, the person setting the energy level, not the one reacting to others' negativity. In this moment, what can you do to raise the energy around you? Perhaps you change the direction of the conversation to a positive topic, compliment someone, or simply smile.

6. Transformation Through Takeoff & Traction

The magic of transformation happens after you've gone through all of the other steps in the FLIGHT Method. True transformation is built on consistently putting the FLIGHT Method into practice. Remember, the runway is where confidence builds; takeoff is when you commit.

At the end of the Transformation Through Takeoff & Traction section in chapter 7, the suggested action was to ask yourself the following questions:

- Did I notice my frequency today?
- Did I let go of at least one resistance?
- Did I choose intentional inputs?
- Did I grow in some way?
- Did I share high-vibe output?

Have you successfully cleared the interference and raised your frequency? If so, great! If not, go through the steps again, notice where you feel resistance, and take intentional action to move past it.

The Power of Situational Awareness

In aviation, we talk about "getting behind the aircraft." It means that the pilot is no longer in control of the situation, and the aircraft's circumstances are outpacing the pilot's ability to manage them. It's that moment when events unfold faster than the pilot's ability to process and respond. When this happens, the pilot shifts from being proactive to reactive. And that can be a dangerous place to be. Poor situational awareness is often called "running around with your hair on fire," and we've all experienced this a time or two—metaphorically, of course!

That's why situational awareness is essential for a pilot. It's the pilot's ability to understand where they are, what's happening, and what's coming next. That awareness is critical to making informed decisions in the face of uncertainty.

Just as a pilot must constantly monitor altitude, airspeed, weather conditions, and aircraft systems to maintain safe flight, you must continuously assess your internal state, emotional responses, and energetic output to stay aligned with your desired outcomes. That's your situational awareness. Without it, your energy and vibration can take a nosedive from something as innocuous as a coworker's offhand comment or hearing a piece of bad news. Before you know it, your emotions are triggered, and you find yourself reacting to your environment instead of proactively responding.

With situational awareness, a pilot stays ahead of the aircraft. They recognize the danger signs and quickly course correct, allowing them to keep flying on track to their destination.

You must also constantly observe your surroundings and be aware of your emotional state. With situational awareness, you stay ahead and maintain your frequency. After all, we can't live our lives wearing garlic necklaces to ward off the energy vampires.

The OODA Loop for Frequency

Military operations depend on what's called the OODA Loop, a four-stage decision-making framework developed by U.S.

Air Force Colonel John Boyd.[19] The framework is meant to help an individual process and react to events in real time. The OODA Loop is also a helpful tool for managing your energy and vibrations. I've adapted it to work with frequency check-ins:

> Observe: Constantly observe your vibrational and energetic state.
> Orient: Orient yourself to what's actually happening versus your perception of events.
> Decide: Choose the frequency adjustment you need to make.
> Act: Make the correction to realign your energy.

After the last step in the loop, act, the process immediately returns to the first step, observing the outcomes of the action, feeding new information into the loop, and allowing for continuous adjustment and refinement. You'll repeat the OODA Loop as often as necessary to raise your frequency throughout the day. At first, going through this loop can seem time-consuming, but when you get good at it, it becomes second nature.

The OODA Loop in Real Life

Even though the OODA Loop was created for the military, it's easy to adapt it to everyday life situations. I'll give you a few examples:

---

19 Brian R. Price, "Colonel John Boyd's Thoughts on Disruption: A Useful Effects Spiral from Uncertainty to Chaos," *Journal of Advanced Military Studies* 14, no. 1 (2024): https://doi.org/10.21140/mcuj.20231401004

Workplace Stress Reset

You are in a meeting that starts to get tense. You *observe* your heart rate speed up and your thoughts begin to race. You *orient* by realizing it's not personal, just a stressful topic. You *decide* to ground yourself by taking a few deep breaths. Then you *act* by doing it. Within minutes, your energy shifts, and you're able to stay calm and respond thoughtfully.

Handling Negativity From Others

You run into a friend at the grocery store, and they start venting about their problems. You *observe* that your previously great mood is turning. You *orient* by recognizing that you're absorbing their energy. You *decide* to stay compassionate without taking on their frequency. You *act* by gently shifting the topic to something lighter.

Another option is to use one of your predetermined exit strategies. You could offer to have a conversation about their issue at a more appropriate time. Or, you might give them a hug and suggest meeting for lunch. Exit strategies allow you to take the time to mentally prepare yourself so that you can be there for your friend without letting the negativity bring your frequency down.

Morning Energy Adjustment

You wake up feeling sluggish and irritable. You *observe* your low energy and vibration. You *orient* by remembering that you stayed up late scrolling through social media. You *decide* to move your body instead of picking up your phone. You *act* by doing ten minutes of stretching and drinking water. As the sun rises outside your window, so does your frequency.

As you can see, if you can remember to Observe, Orient, Decide, and Act, you can switch your energy quickly to keep living at a high frequency.

The Cost of Poor Vibrational Situational Awareness

Just as spatial disorientation can be fatal to a pilot, vibrational disorientation can be devastating to your goals. When you operate without situational awareness, you:

- React instead of respond
- Absorb negative energy
- Project low-frequency emotions onto situations

Essentially, you're flying blind. Instead of heading toward your goals and aspirations, you sabotage your mission through energetic interference.

Developing Energetic Instruments

Effective situational awareness requires systematic scanning and assessment. That's the OODA Loop in action. In addition, you need to develop what I call "energetic instruments"— energetic gauges that help you quickly assess your current vibrational state:

- Emotional barometer: Are you energized or frustrated?
- Tension scanner: Where is the stress showing up in your body?

- Thought-pattern radar: Are your thoughts constructive or destructive?
- Interaction aftermath assessment: Do you feel energetic or drained afterward?

The key is to check your "energetic instruments" often. Just as a pilot scans his instruments frequently, maintaining your frequency requires the same kind of disciplined consideration. Make it a habit to check your instruments several times throughout the day. Soon, checking in with your frequency will become second nature to you.

Maintaining High-Frequency Awareness Under Pressure

In emergencies, training takes over when conscious thought becomes overwhelmed. Your vibrational frequency requires the same kind of disciplined preparation. You need preestablished protocols for common scenarios that cause interference with your frequency.

Develop a standard operating procedure for handling common situations. For instance, criticism, delays, difficult people, or bad news can drain your energy in seconds. You might respond by:

- Taking a deep breath and saying, "Thank you for the feedback."
- Practicing gratitude and reframing negativity into positivity.
- Visualizing yourself easily overcoming the obstacle.
- Using your predetermined exit strategies.

When turbulence hits, you won't have to stop and think about what to do. You won't have to consult the aircraft safety card. Your automatic response will kick in. This type of preparation is Grounded Growth from the FLIGHT Method, and it helps you build resilience through consistent practice.

The Ripple Effect of High-Frequency Situational Awareness

When you maintain consistent awareness of your vibrational state, you become what aviators call "ahead of the aircraft." You anticipate challenges, make smooth adjustments, and inspire confidence in those around you. Your family, friends, and colleagues begin to sense your centered, intentional energy. Opportunities flow to you more easily, and obstacles are resolved more quickly. You become someone who can be trusted to stay calm, positive, and effective under pressure.

Situational awareness is the difference between hope and certainty in achieving your goals. Hope is flying without instruments in cloudy conditions. You simply "hope" you can safely navigate to your destination, and we all know "hope" is not a plan. Certainty is maintaining perfect situational awareness of both your external and internal frequency, making continuous micro-adjustments to stay on course, and reaching your intended destination on time and without incident.

Flying Clear Above the Noise

No matter how much noise surrounds you, remember that you always have the power to clear the interference. Resistance will always show up in the form of people (energy vampires), circumstances, or your own thoughts. But with awareness and practice, you can take steps to quiet the noise and choose to respond in the best possible way.

Situational awareness gives you the clarity to predict turbulent situations before they throw you off course. Every time you check in with your frequency and make intentional adjustments using the OODA Loop, you become better equipped to live a high-frequency life.

Now that you've learned how to clear the interference and fly with awareness, the next challenge is to make sure your frequency stays clear. The best way to do that is to keep things simple. Simplicity is how you stay calm and connected to what matters most.

CHAPTER 10
Simplify Your Signal

Too often in life, we overcomplicate what should be simple. For example, happiness can be found in simple pleasures such as enjoying nature or building friendships. However, people often chase happiness through material possessions or grand gestures.

Society constantly tells us that more is better, that happiness can be found at the bottom of a shopping bag or by adding another award to the trophy wall. We overdo it because we've been conditioned to believe that the more we have and the harder we work for success, the more valuable it must be.

Even in trying to simplify, we tend to miss the mark.

We download the latest apps and buy the newest gadgets, thinking they will solve our problems. Now we have to update the apps, remember passwords, log in, log out. In reality, all we need is a simple calendar or a notebook and some accountability for our tasks.

Self-development is another area where we pursue perfectionism, believing that we have to perform every self-improvement practice flawlessly or hit every goal at 100% accuracy. We think simple solutions lack substance; if the solution is too simple, it won't work.

The truth is that perfectionism, overthinking, and the consequent stress from overcomplicating life drag your frequency down. Every time you pile on another "should," worry or second-guess yourself, your energetic signal gets fuzzy with static.

On the other hand, simplicity raises your frequency. When you simplify, you send a clean, powerful vibration. Your signal goes out clear and strong, and you begin to attract the high-frequency life you're striving for. Simplicity helps quiet the noise and clear the clutter that hinders you from reaching your goals.

But how do you simplify your signal and clear up your frequency and vibration?

To send out a strong, clear signal, you need to let go of the old conditioning that's keeping you stuck, face your fears head-on, and rebuild your self-image.

In the pages that follow, I'll walk you through how to accomplish each of these steps. Some of the thoughts and ideas might feel familiar because we've already touched on them. The reason I'm repeating them here is that repetition is a fundamental building block of learning. Repetition strengthens neural connections, allowing for deeper processing. As you continue working on raising your frequency through the practices in this book, they will become second nature to you.

Let's start with letting go of the old conditioning that's keeping you stuck.

Discard Old Conditioning

From the time you were young, you've been handed beliefs from parents, teachers, peers, and even well-meaning friends. Maybe they thought they were protecting you when they said:

- "Don't aim too high. You'll just be disappointed."
- "It's better to play it safe."
- "People like us don't get opportunities like that."
- "Are you sure that's the right career path for you?"
- "Why don't you just get a real job?"

They may have thought they were helping, but those words planted seeds of doubt. Instead of encouraging you to take the shot, they caused hesitation, stifling your growth and setting you on a trajectory opposite from what you would have chosen.

In chapter 4, we covered limiting beliefs and old conditioning, and how common it is to view the world through a lens of beliefs that don't even belong to you. These beliefs were pressed upon you and absorbed into your psyche until you thought they were part of your identity. Simplifying your signal starts with letting them go.

You can't operate at your highest frequency while holding onto the baggage of old beliefs that don't serve you. It's like having a closet filled with hand-me-down clothes. As you built your wardrobe, well-meaning friends and family members offered what they had. But the clothes aren't your style, and some of them don't even fit. When you box them up and send them away, you open up space for new clothes—clothes that represent your style, fit you well, and look good on you.

Discarding old conditioning works in much the same way. When you clear away the hand-me-down thoughts and beliefs, you make room to create your own beliefs. Beliefs that are aligned with your goals, represent the person you want to be, and look good on you.

What do you choose to believe for yourself? Would you aim higher, even though you might be disappointed? Would you take a risk? Would you let intuition guide you as you make a career choice, instead of listening to what the world says you should choose?

Determine Which Beliefs to Discard

At the end of the section on limiting beliefs in chapter 4, I offered a self-assessment to help you decipher your negative beliefs and determine which one you'll discard first.

It's time to revisit that assessment. Go through the assessment again, answer the questions, and compare your answers to the first time you took it. Have you let go of the biggest limiting belief you struggled with? Are you ready to move to the next one? Make a new goal to focus on one limiting belief and challenge it every time it comes up.

Self-Assessment

1. List your top three negative beliefs. Some examples are:
   » I never have enough time.
   » I never have enough money.
   » I'm not talented enough.

- » I'm too old.
- » I need to be perfect.
- » I'm afraid of failure (or success).

2. Now look at your list and ask yourself:
   - » Which belief shows up the most often in my daily life?
   - » Which one seems to feed into the others? For example, "I need to be perfect" might also fuel the fear of failure or not feeling talented enough.
   - » Which belief holds me back in more than one area of my life? (Relationships, work, health, finances.)
3. The first limiting belief I will challenge is _____.
4. Every time this limiting belief comes up, I'll flip the script by saying _____.

Overcome Fear

Now that you've begun to simplify your signal by letting go of old conditioning, the next step is to overcome fear. In the introduction, I talked about why fear is the number one reason you aren't achieving your dreams.

Remember the skydiving story? Did you feel apprehensive just reading about jumping out of an airplane at 14,000 feet? When you landed safely on the ground, you realized that all of the fear you felt surrounding the jump was just stories you made up in your head. By making the jump and landing safely, you proved that those fears were not real.

You might think that a lack of talent, resources, or opportunities is keeping you stuck. But fear of failure, of the unknown, of not being good enough—that's what keeps you trapped in mediocrity and stranded in the lowest possible vibration.

Fear is False Expectations Appearing Real

Fears are literally just stories you tell yourself. They're fiction. They're not based on facts. Fears are formulated from incomplete information, and they block you from seeing the possibilities.

What would happen if you turned and faced your fears instead of running from them? What would happen if you strapped on your parachute and jumped out of that airplane?

When you face your fears, something magical happens. They lose their power. You begin to see them for what they really are—false expectations appearing real—and your frequency shifts. Now, you deal in knowledge and facts instead of fiction. Instead of asking, "What if it all goes wrong?" you ask, "What if it all goes *right*?"

And that's when the universe conspires to help you succeed.

Remember the Law of Attraction? We covered the 12 Laws in chapter 3. The Law of Attraction says that like attracts like. If you live in fear, you'll attract more things to be afraid of. But when you act with courage and strength, you attract opportunities and resources that match the higher vibration and frequency associated with bravery.

Transform Fear Into Courage

Fear is just energy, and energy can be transformed. That's the Law of Perpetual Transmutation of Energy at work. Energy can be neither created nor destroyed, but can change form. What if you transformed your fear into something better, like courage, creativity, or action?

I'm not saying that you should never feel fearful, anxious, or afraid. Fear is a basic human emotion. Its goal is to protect us from danger. But sometimes, there is no real threat of danger. Most often, fear is false. That's your opportunity to feel the emotion of fear, and do it anyway. Because on the other side of fear is a completely different version of you. The version that is courageous and successful. The one who takes action, even when it feels scary.

A popular phrase thrown around in the self-development world is, "Get out of your comfort zone." But I say, "Get out of your *fear* zone." When you break through fear, even one fear, you don't just overcome that one thing. You raise your entire vibrational frequency. Your subconscious learns that you're capable of more. And then you do more because new opportunities are now waiting for you.

Let's talk about one fear held by many: the fear of public speaking. In our modern digital world, this fear translates into the fear of going live on social media. So, let's use going live on social media as an example of how to identify and overcome your fear.

1. Identify one fear that's been holding you back. Example: I'm afraid of going live on Instagram because I might forget what I'm saying and embarrass myself.
2. Gather the facts and replace the false story with real information. Example: The truth is, most people don't

expect perfection on live streams. My audience isn't watching to judge me. They watch to learn or be inspired.
3. Take one small action toward overcoming the fear. Example: Go live for just one minute to share a short tip. Or practice by recording what you want to say before you post it.
4. Visualize yourself doing the scary thing. Example: Picture yourself hitting the button to go live, smiling into the camera, and delivering your thoughts with confidence. In your mind, see your audience's positive comments filling the screen.
5. Feel the emotions when you succeed. Example: Imagine ending the live stream, smiling, and feeling proud, energized, and excited to do it again. Positive emotions lock in a higher frequency for next time.

Overcoming fear simplifies your signal by creating a more powerful frequency. Now, let's take the next step by building a new self-image.

Build a New Self-Image

Once you recognize the way your old conditioning and fears have been directing your life, it sets the stage to begin building your new self-image. This is where the magic happens because when you see yourself differently, you see the possibilities that await you.

The biggest key to building your new self-image is reprogramming your subconscious mind. It's like upgrading your operating system. The old system is slow, buggy, and prone to crashing. But the upgrade is faster and capable of running programs you couldn't run before. When you update your self-image, you unlock capabilities you didn't have access to with the old software.

Three Steps to Building a New Self-Image

The old operating system was filled with limiting beliefs and old conditioning. The new, updated system is created through intentional input, visualization, and believing you already are the person you wish to be.

1. Operate with Intention

It would be great if we could snap our fingers and conjure up a shiny new self-image. But it doesn't work that way. Your self-image is rebuilt through intentional self-development practices. What you consume shapes who you become. The more you immerse yourself in personal growth through books, podcasts, mentors, and practices, the more you train your subconscious mind to operate at higher frequencies.

2. See Your Future

Before you can rebuild your self-image, you have to know what you want to become. Use meditation and visualization practices to picture the person you want to be. Imagine yourself already living the life you want. Visualization signals to your subconscious that you're ready to move in that direction.

3. Act As If

Your subconscious mind learns through repetition, imagery, and action. If you want to become a confident leader, start by practicing your leadership skills in small groups. Small, intentional actions anchor your new self-image in the real world. Over time, your subconscious mind aligns with your vision of your future self. It starts believing the new reality you've created, and once it does, your actions, habits, and results follow. That's how you build a new self-image.

Becoming Who You Want to Be

You may wonder if discarding old conditioning, overcoming fear, and building a new self-image are worth the time and effort that it takes to remove those roadblocks and simplify your signal. Once you realize what you are capable of, everything changes. You'll naturally attract the identity you've been searching for. Everything will start to align, and your subconscious will know that there are no limits to what you can do; you can create anything you want.

Simplifying your signal clears away the noise. The old conditioning, the fear, and the self-doubt are replaced with clarity, courage, and a new, stronger self-image. When your signal is clear, you no longer send out mixed signals. Instead, you broadcast at a higher frequency of strength, purpose, and possibility.

In the next chapter, we'll learn how to activate your frequency so the signal you send out resonates far and wide, attracting the life you've envisioned.

CHAPTER 11
Activate Your Frequency

How many times have you said to yourself, "I'll start when I have more time...when I have more money or access to resources...when things settle down...when I finish this project?" But when that time comes, something else pops up. So you keep putting it off and putting it off. You never make tangible progress on your goals. Not only is this vicious cycle painful, but it actually breeds more resistance.

If you want to reach your goals and attract the desires of your heart, you have to activate your frequency. You have to push play and start. And the FLIGHT Method helps you do that.

As a reminder, here's the framework we covered in chapter 7:

1. Frequency Awareness
2. Let Go of Resistance
3. Intentional Input
4. Grounded Growth
5. High-Vibe Output
6. Transformation Through Take Off & Traction

To take FLIGHT, you first become aware of your current frequency. Next, you let go of resistance. And then you begin taking action intentionally. As you take action, you become grounded in growth, which raises your frequency to a higher level of output.

When you take any step toward your dreams, no matter how small, you activate the frequency that helps you manifest it, and that activation begins with becoming aware of your frequency.

But the most important step for frequency activation is Intentional Input. The Law of Inspired Action says that the universe responds to movement. That means the single decision to take action, however small, is the spark that propels you into motion. Once you're in motion, momentum carries you forward.

Waiting until everything in your life is perfectly aligned doesn't just stall progress; it lowers your frequency. Not starting keeps you stuck and stagnant. And that can be frustrating. Taking the first step, no matter how small, is the action that sparks energy and activates higher frequency and vibration.

Picture yourself going to the gym. On the days you don't feel like working out, it's hard to make yourself go. But once you walk in the door and start warming up, you overcome the resistance (Let Go of Resistance). The warm-up (Intentional Input) gives you the little push you need, building momentum to keep going and finish your workout. At the end, you feel a sense of accomplishment (Grounded Growth), and your positive energy lifts those around you (High-Vibe Output).

The first step, the initial push, leads right into the next step. It creates the momentum to build a consistent practice. Consistency is built through daily practice, even when you don't feel like it. Random bursts of effort won't get you there. Frequency activation doesn't happen in the wishing and waiting. It happens in the doing, and consistency is key.

The Frequency Mirror

Energy is contagious. Whether you know it or not, you influence the environment around you every single day. Your energy can either raise people up or drag them down. The question is, are you setting the vibration you want to live, or simply reacting to the frequency set by others?

You don't attract what you *want*; you attract what you *are*. Life reflects your frequency back to you. If you walk around sending out vibrations of scarcity and fear, you'll find situations and people who match those vibrations. But if you radiate gratitude, joy, and confidence, the same law applies. Remember the Law of Cause and Effect (Karma)? It's like a boomerang. Anything you send out will return to you. So if you're living a high-frequency life, sending out good vibrations, you'll draw in the people and experiences that resonate with those higher frequencies.

If you search online, you can find a powerful video that demonstrates resonance with tuning forks. A tuning fork is a two-pronged metal instrument that produces a pure note when the tines are struck. The two prongs vibrate at a set rate, which is the fork's frequency. Tuning forks come in different sizes, each with its own individual frequency.

Now this is the interesting part...when you strike a tuning fork and hold it near a second tuning fork tuned to the same frequency, the second fork will begin resonating without ever touching it. The vibrations from the first fork travel through space and activate the second. And that's exactly how your frequency works. The energy you send out sets other energies in motion, whether you realize it or not. That's why it's important to activate the frequency you want to resonate with.

So, how do you activate your frequency? You put into action a few simple practices.

Frequency Activators

Chapter 8 was filled with practices to sustain high-frequency living. But the goal of this chapter is to help you start activating your frequency right now with quick, simple actions. These frequency activators can be done anytime, anywhere. There are a few mindset shifts that help you build momentum as you dive into the practices from chapter 8.

Here are four things you can do to activate your frequency right now.

1. Be Grateful

Practicing gratitude instantly raises your vibration, but most people don't use it correctly. They only turn to gratitude when life isn't going well. They use it as an emergency lever to pull when a truckload of lemons gets dumped on their doorstep. But gratitude works best when it becomes a daily practice—and it's easy to build gratitude into your day. For example, before you start your day, name three things, big or small, that you're grateful for. Throughout the day, pause and acknowledge something that's going well. In the evening, reflect on the good things that happened and express gratitude for them. When built into your daily routine, gratitude becomes part of your new self-image, not just something you do when times get tough.

2. Let Go of Limiting Beliefs

Limiting beliefs are the negative thoughts or perceptions you hold that keep you from reaching your full potential. The interesting thing is that many of your limiting beliefs did not originate with you. The thought that you're not good enough, the pattern of not following through with your goals, and the fear of failure may all be results of the opinions of others or past negative experiences. Those old scripts shaped your self-image beginning in childhood, and that self-image has shaped your current frequency. When you let go of the limiting beliefs and replace them with positive beliefs and prosperity consciousness, you rebuild your self-image and reshape your frequency. If you need a refresher on limiting beliefs, revisit obstacle #1 in chapter 4.

3. Boost Your Frequency

At any time, in any place, you can boost your frequency with a simple action. These are simple actions that require almost no effort, but create massive shifts in your energy. Keep a few of these instant frequency boosters ready to employ:

- Smile and greet people. Remember, your energy introduces you before you ever say a word.

- Say thank you. When gratitude is spoken out loud, it multiplies in frequency.
- Hold a door for someone. Showing simple kindness to those you interact with elevates the energy in the interaction.
- Do something kind for someone you don't know with nothing expected in return.
- Turn negative energy around. When you encounter negative energy from someone else, whether in real life or online, resist the temptation to match their frequency. Instead, smile and find something positive to focus on.

As you practice these frequency boosters, pay attention to how each small action elevates your energy. Notice how quickly positive energy expands when you're intentional.

4. Expect Success

Several years ago, when I first began working for myself, I struggled to have even a small amount of success. My mentor, the person who introduced me to personal development, called one day and asked me if I knew why I wasn't having success.

"I don't know," I replied.

He informed me that the reason I was not having success was that I didn't expect it.

"Steve," he said, "If you want success, you have to *expect* that you'll be successful."

My first reaction was to argue and defend myself. Of course I expect success. That's why I'm putting so much energy into this.

But instead of arguing, I thought about what he said. I took a look at how I was portraying myself and my product to my customers. He was right. I did not expect to have success because I had been marketing a product that deep down, I didn't expect people to buy. My belief in myself was not strong enough for me to see people actually getting involved with what I had to offer.

This is a perfect example of the subconscious mind giving me exactly what I asked for. I had given my energy to the fact that people would not purchase this product based on my old conditioning. I told myself, "It's too expensive; people are not going to spend this much." Essentially, I chose for them.

Remember, what you give energy to is what the subconscious sees as reality. The subconscious only knows what you tell it. My subconscious heard me telling it that I expected to fail. So, my subconscious mind said, "He's asking to fail, he expects to fail, so that's what I'll give him."

At that moment, I changed my attitude and my mindset about my business. What I had been missing all along was confidence. Once I realized confidence was the key to being a successful leader, I began to see success materialize in my life.

The next month, my business made $35,000 in profit within 30 days. Expecting success made all the difference in the world.

To have success in any area of your life takes more than a few universal laws and some personal development. All the personal development in the world will not help you if you don't believe in yourself. You have to expect the success you seek.

This is where most people get it backward. They want to have success before they've done the work to become the type of person who is successful. They say, "Once I have success, I'll feel confident and grateful."

But frequency doesn't work that way. What you put out is what comes back. To achieve success, you first have to be confident and grateful, and then act as if you are successful. Success follows expectation, not the other way around.

Think of it in terms of this simple formula: Be, Do, Have. *Be* the person you want to be, *do* the things that a successful person would do, and then you'll *have* the things a successful person has.

For instance, when you step into the gym expecting a great workout, you create the conditions in your subconscious mind to complete a killer workout. When you head into a business meeting expecting to win over the client, you carry yourself differently, and others respond to that energy. Expectation is confidence in motion, and it's one of the best frequency activators.

Practice Activating Your Frequency

Now it's your turn to practice activating your frequency. For the next 14 days, commit to activating your frequency every single day. Here's how:

1. Pick one to two small actions each day. Start with one of the easy frequency activators from this chapter, or begin one of the practices we talked about in chapter 8.

2. Track your progress. Journal about your experiences each night. What did you notice about your energy? How did people respond to you?
3. Share your wins. Post about your experiences in the Frequency of Success Facebook Group. Share how these daily activations changed your interactions, mindset, or results.

The goal of this challenge is to help you push play. It's all about just getting started. Zig Ziglar said, "You don't have to be great to start, but you have to start to be great."[20]

So stop waiting! Don't wait for the perfect time. Don't wait until you feel ready. Decide now to begin.

---

20 "Zig Ziglar Quotes," *BrainyQuote*, accessed December 11, 2025. https://www.brainyquote.com/quotes/zig_ziglar_617778.

CONCLUSION
Ready to Take FLIGHT

You've made it!

You've cleared the interference, simplified your signal, and activated your frequency. You've learned how to check your energy and vibration, and how to take action to tune up your frequency. You've done the inner work and built habits that prepare you for an extraordinary high-frequency life.

Now, you're cleared for takeoff!

The work you've done throughout these pages has provided you with the lessons and practices meant to give you your wings. The question is, when you close this book, will you keep your frequency high? Will you fly?

The FLIGHT So Far

Let's take a moment to look back on how far you've come.

In part 1, you discovered that your energy determines your results. You saw how every thought, emotion, and belief carries a vibration, and that the frequency you operate from directly shapes your success. You learned that it's not just about working harder; it's about consistency too. You explored the 12 Universal Laws, gaining a deeper understanding of how the universe responds to your energy and vibration. You faced the internal and external obstacles that threw you off course. And you learned how to recognize interference.

In part 2, you found out what it's like to step into the cockpit and pilot your aircraft. You explored the FLIGHT Method and how it brings purpose and structure to your transformation. You learned practices to help you sustain high-frequency living like gratitude, mindfulness, meditation, and visualization. You also learned that raising your vibration isn't just a mental game; it's physical as well. Providing your body with proper nutrition and rest is essential.

And in part 3, you learned how to clear the interference that drains your energy. You simplified your signal by discarding old conditioning and overcoming fear. And finally, you learned how to activate your frequency with frequency activators like practicing gratitude.

And don't forget about the My Vibrational Frequency Self-Assessment Test at the end of chapter 2. Now that you've finished the book, it's time to take the assessment again to see how far you've come. This is a tool you can use again and again. I recommend taking it every month at first as you begin to build up your frequency of success muscles.

Now, you have everything you need to fly higher and live with more purpose and success than ever before. But just knowing is not enough. There's more.

The Real Work Begins

Here's what I want you to remember: The amount of effort it took you to become successful will not keep you there. You have to keep doing the work. I'm talking about consistency and lifelong learning.

Anyone can read a book, do affirmations for 21 days, and see some level of positive change. But as I showed you in chapter 6, those types of hollow practices don't initiate real change. It's only when you consistently tune in with high-frequency thoughts and actions that you move the needle.

Think of consistency as the engine that keeps your plane in the air. You can't rev up your engines, take off, and then cut the engine and expect to coast forever. You have to keep doing the work, even when turbulence hits or when you can't see the horizon. Watch your gauges, maintain altitude, and keep making steady adjustments. You have to show up even when it's not convenient because the results come only with persistence.

Confidence and Consistency Go Hand in Hand

The secret sauce to maintaining consistency is to have confidence in yourself. When you trust yourself to keep showing up, keep raising your frequency day after day, your energy changes. You start believing in your ability to block interference when it comes knocking.

But what if you lack confidence? What if you're still trying to let go of those limiting beliefs that whisper you're not good enough? Or that you don't deserve to succeed?

The good news is that confidence is something you can borrow. We talked about borrowing confidence before, and it might sound funny because it's not like your overconfident friend can just hand you a box of confidence. You can't go on Amazon and buy it. But if you've ever pretended to have confidence in the face of fear, you know what I mean.

It goes back to the idea of "act as if." Act as if you're already confident. Act as if you're already successful. Acting confident, even if it feels foreign to you, helps you align with the version of yourself who is confident. Because that person exists. You just haven't grown into that person yet.

If you knew you couldn't fail, how would you live? What would you wear? What type of car would you drive? What would your home feel like?

If you knew you couldn't fail, would you quit?

No, you wouldn't. Because the person who *knows* they can't fail never stops striving for more. And that is a high-frequency mindset. It's where confidence eats, sleeps, lives, and breathes.

Maybe you already know all of this. If you do, that's great! You are going to have an incredible life. For me, it took a wise flight examiner and almost failing my flight test to find confidence in my ability to fly.

Finding the Confidence to Fly

Two areas in my life far exceed all other areas for the amount of passion and confidence I have. One is flying airplanes, and the other is skydiving. However, just to let you know, I never do them both at the same time.

As a professional pilot, I have over 16,500 hours of flight time and over 31 years of experience. As a skydiver, I have over 17,000 jumps. But I didn't always have the kind of confidence I have now.

When I was hired for my first job as a passenger charter pilot, I had to take a check-ride with an examiner from the Federal Aviation Administration. It's similar to taking your driver's test, only the examiners are not nearly as friendly. The day I was scheduled to take my check-ride, I was very nervous, as this was my first real job.

I finished the three-hour oral exam easily, and then went out to the airplane for the flight portion. When a pilot takes a check-ride for a charter pilot job, they fly most of the one to three-hour flight portion under what is called a hood. This means flying without being able to see out the window, flying strictly by reference to the flight instruments.

As I began this portion of my check-ride, I felt nervous. About 30 minutes into the flight, I found myself making mistakes that I normally did not make. Somewhere around the third or fourth mistake, the examiner said, "Why don't we go on back to the airport and talk about this?" I knew right then the ride was over; I had failed. Everything felt over. My time in college—wasted. My student loan debt—for nothing. My dream of becoming a professional pilot—crushed.

When we got back to the airport, we went into the conference room and the examiner said, "You know what your problem is? You've got no confidence. You're a great pilot and you know what you're doing; you just don't have the confidence to do it." He went on to say, "I'd suggest you put a little chip on your shoulder and fly like you know how, or you're going to kill yourself and possibly someone else."

The examiner told me he was going to grab some lunch and when he came back, we would do the flight portion again, and he did not want to see the same person flying.

While he was gone, I thought about the advice he had given me. The more I thought about his words, the more I realized he was right. I really was a good pilot, and I didn't have to second-guess myself.

After lunch, we went back to the airplane and took off for the flight portion. The entire flight took about two hours and went perfectly. I flew better than I had ever flown before. During the first flight, I had let fear creep into my mind, which made me question my own abilities. Now, it felt so good to know that I had the power and skill within me all along. It's like Glinda the Good Witch in *The Wizard of Oz* telling Dorothy that she always had the power to go home, she just had to learn for herself how to tap into that power. That confidence has since carried over into my business and personal life and has been a huge factor in my successes.

To this day, the examiner's advice has been some of the most valuable guidance I have ever received. It not only made me a better pilot, but it has also made me a better person all around, for it applies to virtually all areas of my life.

Now, I want you to think about your life. What area of your life are you most confident in? What area are you least confident in? Where would you like to see your confidence grow? For example, maybe you would like to be better at sales, or perhaps you want to be more confident in investing.

Now here's the secret: It is not necessary for you to know all the answers to have the confidence you seek. The important thing to remember is that confidence comes from you and no one else.

If you're thinking, "But Steve, how do I get confidence if I don't have it in me?" The answer is simple. You act as if you do. You trick yourself into having the confidence you desire. Don't be Dorothy, waiting for Glinda. Find your inner power now.

How to Find Confidence

Remember when I said your confident friend can't just give you a box of confidence? Well, that's true, but there's another way you can borrow their confidence.

Try this: take out a piece of paper and draw a line down the middle, lengthwise, so you have two columns. At the top of the left column, write "Successful Person." At the top of the right column, write "Me."

In the left column, list all the qualities you believe a confident, successful person has. Think about your confident friend, a mentor, or someone you look up to. Here are some qualities you might list:

- Self-assured

- Authentic
- Resilient
- Optimistic
- Disciplined
- Focused
- Calm under pressure
- Empathetic
- Decisive
- Purpose-driven

As you list qualities, challenge yourself to come up with every possible trait a confident person would have. Begin to build this person in your mind. How would this person walk? How would they talk? What would they wear? How would they carry themselves in a group setting?

Once you have a list of 10 to 20 traits that you believe describe the perfect confident person, ask yourself if you have any of those qualities. Copy the ones that apply to you over to the "Me" column. You'll probably be surprised at how many overlap.

Now, what about the qualities you don't have? These are the qualities you want to develop. So, how do you learn and develop them? You invest in yourself.

Invest in Your Confidence

If you've made it this far, you've already proven that you're serious about personal growth. You've invested the cost of this book, plus your time to read it and take the assessments. But don't stop there!

To keep your energy fresh and your vibration high, you need to refresh your mind with new information. You need to surround yourself with high-frequency people. That's how you continue to be grounded in growth.

Here are a few ways to live a high-frequency life:

- Read every day. Fill your mind with ideas that expand your knowledge and awareness.
- Build your personal development library. But don't just collect new books. Take time to study and learn.
- Invest in experiences. Attend masterclasses, retreats, and live events that motivate, teach, and inspire you.
- Surround yourself with people who are going where you want to go. Remember, we are like the people we surround ourselves with.

The more you invest in yourself and your growth, the more your energy will expand and the higher your frequency will fly. And results will follow; it's the universal laws at play.

How to Stay Connected

You've cleared the runway, fueled your mind, body, and spirit, and tuned your instruments. Your pre-flight check is complete. Now it's time to trust your wings and fly high with purpose.

This may be the end of the book, but it's only the beginning of all the opportunities and possibilities waiting for you. And the best part about living a high-frequency life is doing it with others who are flying at the same altitude. Remember: The most important investment you'll ever make is the investment you make in yourself!

The Frequency of Success Website

Visit http://www.TheFrequencyofSuccess.com to explore upcoming events, coaching programs, online courses, and resources designed to keep you tuned in to higher frequencies. You'll find the tools, inspiration, and support you need to keep your results soaring.

The Frequency of Success Facebook Group

I started the Frequency of Success Facebook Group so that people like you, those who are committed to living at a higher vibration, can:

- Ask questions
- Get advice for growth
- Connect with like-minded individuals
- Celebrate wins
- Find accountability

We would love to see your growth and cheer you on during your journey.

Just as a rising tide lifts all ships, surrounding yourself with a strong community of high-frequency thinkers will elevate your own energy and momentum. You don't have to fly solo; we're here to be your wingman.

Join the group at https://www.Facebook.com/FrequencyExpert/

Come to a Live Event

Nothing compares to the energy of attending a live experience. When you step into a room filled with high-frequency people, you'll feel your own vibration rise instantly. And it stays with you long after you leave. Visit the Frequency of Success website for information on upcoming dates, event details, and special promotions.

THIS IS YOUR PILOT SPEAKING

Thank you for flying the Frequency of Success Airways today. It's been an honor to share this journey with you, and I look forward to seeing you again soon.

Oh, and if you want to know what it feels like to jump out of an airplane at 14,000 feet, I know a guy…call me!

ABOUT THE AUTHOR: STEVE LINTON

Steve Linton is a pilot, skydiver, speaker, and success coach with over 31 years of flying experience and over 17,000 skydiving jumps to his name. Steve brings a unique perspective on what happens when courage and overcoming fear converge—both in the air and in life.

Early in his career, Steve experienced financial instability, but, determined to change his circumstances, he took the advice of a friend and mentor and began practicing and living according to the 12 Universal Laws. He discovered that success was less about the effort he put forth and more about upgrading the frequency, energy, and vibration he sent out into the world. Once he began to transform his self-image and live as if he were destined for more, he experienced a seismic shift that changed everything. Steve went from struggling to pay the bills to eventually earning over $100,000 in one month consistently as an entrepreneur.

From this lived experience, Steve developed the Frequency of Success philosophy and the FLIGHT Method—a practical framework that blends mindset, energetic alignment, and intentional action to help people create results without burnout.

As a speaker and success coach, Steve is known for his energetic, motivational, and deeply engaging approach. He brings a contagious enthusiasm to his teaching, helping people believe in what's possible for themselves—often before they truly believe it on their own.

Steve lives in Arizona and continues to teach, speak, and help others overcome fear and limiting beliefs, while guiding them to harness the power of inspired action for aligned, exponential growth.

Made in the USA
Coppell, TX
25 February 2026

72320054R00115